W9-BSA-742

ALSO BY PICO IYER

Video Night in Kathmandu

The Lady and the Monk

Falling Off the Map

Cuba and the Night

Tropical Classical

The Global Soul

Abandon

Sun After Dark

The Open Road

THE MAN WITHIN MY HEAD

The Man Within My Head

Pico Iyer

ALFRED A. KNOPF  NEW YORK 2012

THIS IS A BORZOI BOOK

PUBLISHED BY ALFRED A. KNOPF

Copyright © 2012 by Pico Iyer

All rights reserved. Published in the United States by Alfred A. Knopf,
a division of Random House, Inc., New York, and in Canada by
Random House of Canada Limited, Toronto.

www.aaknopf.com

Knopf, Borzoi Books, and the colophon are registered trademarks of
Random House, Inc.

Library of Congress Cataloging-in-Publication Data
Iyer, Pico.
The man within my head / Pico Iyer.
p. cm.
"This is a Borzoi book"—T.p. verso.
ISBN: 978-0-307-26761-0 (hardcover)
1. Greene, Graham, 1904–1991—Influence. 2. Greene, Graham,
1904–1991—Criticism and interpretation. 3. Novelists, English—
20th century—Biography. 4. Iyer, Pico—Family. 5. Fathers and sons.
6. Iyer, Pico—Travel. I. Title.
PR6013.R44Z6344 2012
823'.912—dc23
[B]   2011041285

Jacket images: (top) Graham Greene sitting at his desk, by Sylvia Salmi,
Bettmann/Corbis; (bottom) courtesy of the author;
(dots) Sophie Broadbridge/Getty Images
Jacket design by Abby Weintraub and Carol Devine Carson

Manufactured in the United States of America

FIRST EDITION

What means the fact—which is so common—so universal—that some soul that has lost all hope for itself can inspire in another listening soul an infinite confidence in it, even while it is expressing its despair?

—HENRY DAVID THOREAU *to Lucy Brown,*
January 24, 1843

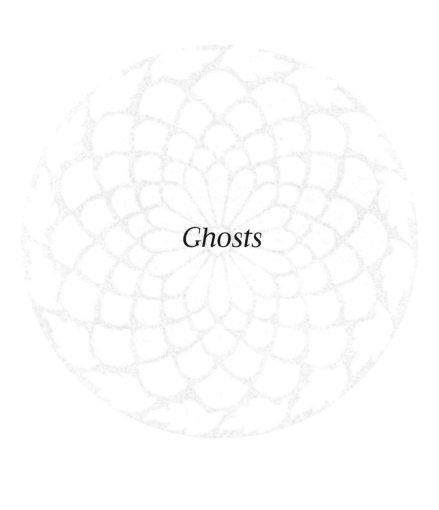

Ghosts

CHAPTER 1

I was standing by the window in the Plaza Hotel, looking out. Below—ten stories below—I could make out round-faced women in ponchos standing on the sidewalk of the city named for peace and renting out cellphones to passersby. At their sides, sisters (or could it be daughters?) were sitting next to mountainous piles of books, mostly advising pedestrians on how to win a million dollars. Along the flower-bordered strip of green that cuts through Bolivia's largest metropolis, a soldier was leading his little girl by the hand, pointing out Mickey and Minnie in Santa's sleigh.

The skies were tumultuous this midsummer afternoon. In parts of the city it seemed to be raining, and shacks cowered under shades of grey and black; in others, great shafts of light broke through the swollen clouds as if to announce some heavenly arrival. Young couples brushed shoulders as they sauntered down a narrow boulevard at whose end seemed to loom a snowcap, rising to nineteen thousand feet. Everything seemed small, distinctly fragile in this elemental landscape.

I drew the curtains and fumbled my way across to my bed. I

fell asleep erratically, constantly in this thin-aired climate, and
when I emerged, I stepped out of dreams of a many-chambered intensity I seldom knew at sea level. I couldn't tell if
a minute had passed—or an hour—when I got up now, but
as I scrambled out of my bed, I made my way to the desk
in one corner and began to write, unstoppably. I had nothing I needed to write—I'd come here seeking a break from
my desk—but now the words came out of me as if someone
(something) had a message urgently to convey.

A boy is standing by a window at his school—this is what I
began to transcribe—as the last parental car disappears down
the driveway. He goes back to his bed and tries to prepare
himself for the next twelve weeks of what can seem like hand-
to-hand combat in some medieval campaign. It's no good feeling sorry for yourself; that will give the others an opening. He
has to use the only thing he has—his mind—to conquer the
environment around him.

Twelve weeks isn't so long, he thinks; it's only eighty-four
days. And twenty-one days ago doesn't seem so long at all. He
just has to go through that four times. Besides, three days is
nothing, and if he can endure that twenty-eight times . . .

But things will not be so easy this term. In the holidays
a friend of his mother's—from her school, a hundred years
ago—had come to visit and the mothers (knowing nothing)
had suggested he play with the woman's son. But the boy
turned out to be a classmate of his, so now both of them were
scarred by an association. It was hard enough to protect just
yourself.

Around him, as he tries to magick the numbers down, come
the sounds of everyday. Boys are sniffling under their covers, and he can hear others tiptoeing across to another bed

to whisper something to an ally. A master paces outside, his steps recalling to them the tennis shoe he's ready to use on any malefactor. The previous Sunday a man from Salisbury had come to chapel and said that all of them had a Father in Heaven who was waiting to admit them to Eternity. But every father he knows has just vanished down the driveway, and Eternity is precisely what he's trying to make go away.

∴

What was going on here? I put down my pen and stared at what I'd done, as if it were something I'd found rather than composed. I'd been at a school akin to this thirty years before—the emotions weren't entirely foreign to me—but why was the main character in the sketch called "Greene," as if he had something to do with the long-dead English novelist? Graham Greene had written, near the end of his life, about how he lay in bed at school and tried to face down the "twelve endless weeks till the holidays"; he sometimes wrote to his American mistress that he was counting down the days till they met, as if he was in school again.

But school had mostly nurtured in him a longing to be alone and a sympathy for the oppressed. Why couldn't I have used the name "Brown"—or "Black" or "White" or "Grey"?

A knock came on the door, and I opened up to see a middle-aged chamberman staring back at me, extending a tank of oxygen. He'd appeared at my door three hours before, impassive under his mop of dark hair, with a tray of candies in the shape of watermelon slices. Was it the ten thousand feet altitude that made me not myself like this? The five or six cups of coca tea

I'd drunk this morning, from the thermos set out in the lobby to help newcomers adjust to the heady atmosphere?

Why had I suddenly remembered, this morning, how my father once, eyes alight and unfailingly magnetic, had broken into torrents of infectious laughter when the Mother Abbess in *The Sound of Music* had burst into "Climb Every Mountain"? Forty years on, in a very different land, I'd heard myself do the same at exactly the same point in the story.

I looked down again and saw the name in my handwriting: "Greene." The novelist had never even come to Bolivia, so far as I knew. Was it only through another that I could begin to get at myself?

∴

I drew back the curtains and, as the light came in, recalled that the same thing, weirdly, had happened three years before, pretty much to the day: I'd taken my mother to Easter Island, at the end of the last millennium, so we could get away from frenzied talk about Y2K in the presence of stone enigmas casting long shadows across great patches of grass. Though far from Catholic ourselves, we'd decided to go to Sunday Mass in a little church in the main town: how often would we get to see a service on Easter Island? Pretty altar girls walked down the aisles, dipping blue collection bags in front of us, as if foraging for goldfish. A priest at the front threw his arms out so we could see the rongorongo symbols on his white robe. Jesus above the altar hung outstretched as if he were just another stone totem, commanding respect with his silences.

We headed back to our simple motel, set beside the black

volcanic rocks against which the surf pounded and subsided, with nothing to be felt but Pitcairn Island, thirteen hundred miles away. My mother retired to take a nap; I, for no reason I could tell, went out to the green lawns behind our sliding doors, bringing a chair from my nearly empty room, and began to write. About a young man in Italy who becomes a priest, dreaming of bringing comfort to the afflicted and light to the darker places in the world. He's sent to the Pacific, famously fertile ground for missionaries, and there, very soon, on Easter Island, he gets converted himself, till soon he is sitting on a terrace with his cocktail, while the children he has made with a pretty island girl play around his feet. His only hope is that Rome will never find out.

Morality is a free-and-easy thing on the island, with none of the hard edges he's hoped to bring to it; his main business is making sure his happy-go-lucky brother-in-law doesn't get into more trouble than he might. When a foreign woman approaches him, to complain that the boy has tried to trick her into an unwanted closeness, it is this unorthodox priest's job to talk her down, by speaking with scrupulous vagueness of the Holy Spirit and its relation to the stone heads all around. His years of theological training have led only, it seems, to a shady (but invaluable) gift for using the unknown to protect the friendly souls around him from themselves.

It wasn't a story I'd taken consciously—or unconsciously— from anyone; it was inspired by this unworldly island. But if I'd shown it to my mother, she'd have said, "This renegade priest with his young girl and tropical lifestyle: isn't this just a version of Graham Greene?"

∴

Graham Greene—his first name was, in fact, Henry—was born in 1904, in the unremarkable English Home Counties town of Berkhamsted. In later years, quite typically, he would recall an inn in the town called the "Crooked Billet" and claim that faces in his birthplace wore "a slyness about the eyes, an unsuccessful cunning." He would remember the rambling house of his uncle Graham, one of the founders of Naval Intelligence, in which he spent summer holidays, a house "very suited to games of hide and seek." Most of all he recalled the many terrors of his boyhood—of darkness, of strangers' footsteps, of houses burning down.

The fourth of six children—and third son—of a schoolmaster, he spent his early days on the grounds of the all-boys school where his father would later become headmaster; thus the Byzantine rules and shifting insurgencies of school shaped—and haunted—him more than they might any other boy. He would have gotten bullied anyway, no doubt, as a shy, painfully sensitive teenager who was bad at games and loved to hide out with his books, but as the son of the head man he was trapped whichever way he turned: if he went along with his classmates and their games of rebellion, he'd be betraying his father (and his upstanding elder brother, who became head boy); but if he walked through the green baize door in the corridor that led to his parents' quarters, he'd be turning his back on his peers and ensuring for himself a traitor's fate. He emerged from school, not surprisingly, with uneasy feelings about authority (on both sides of the door) and the overanxious tremors of one able to see both sides of any question, though likely to commit himself to neither.

His mother, also a Greene, was first cousin to Robert Louis Stevenson, and her father was an Anglican clergyman who suffered from an excess of guilt and defrocked himself in a field; his father's father was a manic-depressive who was buried in St. Kitts, where the man's brother was said to have fathered thirteen children before his death at nineteen. At the age of sixteen, and apparently on the recommendation of his elder brother, a medical student, Greene, having tried and failed to run away from school, was allowed—remarkably for his time and class—to go to live with a therapist in London, Kenneth Richmond, and the man's unsettlingly attractive wife, Zoë. While his classmates were dutifully reciting the Pater Noster and thronging around one another with details of the Hundred Years' War, Greene's only duty was to read history, and to describe his dreams every morning to the Jungian, probing his hidden selves as he told the shadow father, not without apprehension, how he had dreamed of the glamorous Zoë the night before.

Decades later, in a memoir, he would describe his six months in this alternative home—twice—as "the happiest period of my life." Again and again, in his fiction, a young male protagonist is spirited away from home and from school, to disappear into a half-lit underground world, guarded by a kind of unofficial father and his moll. Greene's training at the hands of the unorthodox spiritualist seems to have recalled to him how much in the world extends beyond our grasp, even if we long for certainty and conviction.

His peers at Berkhamsted were learning strength and how to go out and administer Empire, already in its first stages of dissolution. Greene, meanwhile, was learning the opposite: how to take power apart, how to do justice to its victims, on both sides of the fence, how to make a home in his life for pain and even fear. As classmates set about making the official history of their people, he began picking at its secret life, its tremblings, its wounds.

He often dreamed, he would later recall, of his father, "shut away in hospital, out of touch with his wife and children." Sometimes, in the recurring boyhood dreams, his father came home on a visit, "a silent solitary man, not really cured, who would have to go back again into exile." And yet, he wrote in the same book, it was only in dreams, much later, that "his bruised love and sorrow for his dead father sometimes came to him." In later years, his companion Yvonne would write, Greene's own life would start, eerily, to resemble his early dreams of his father.

∴

The high, thin light was turning the shacks and shanties on the hills to gold as I put my thoughts of Greene behind me; La Paz was an ironist's delight with its defiance of all reason. The poor had the best views here, overlooking the bowl-shaped valley of light, while the rich cowered below, not far from the wild rock formations of the Valley of the Moon. Just down the street from me, at the main church, the decorations on its façade, fashioned by Indians pressed into service by their Catholic overlords, swarmed with indigenous runes and subversive symbols; even now, during the twelve days of Christmas, the faithful were walking past the church entrance, up the steep slopes, to where they could buy llama fetuses from witch doctors and aphrodisiacs to win the hearts of obstinate strangers.

The previous day, I'd traveled out to the town's main cemetery, under a ridge of huts, and seen a monkey in a cage, with a coat on, handing out pieces of folded white paper—fortunes, I assumed—to members of the crowd that had gathered round him. Inside the city of the dead, a middle-aged man was patiently washing the windows of a drawer-like compartment in one of the multistory cabinets in which the departed lay, a red rose in front of most of their openings. Lovers stretched out on the grass next to huge sepulchres, enjoying the one spot in the city where their whispers would not be drowned out by the roar of passing buses. From somewhere along the long rows of cabinets, where Indian women rented out blue ladders for those whose loved ones were on higher floors, I could just make out a scratchy transistor radio, "Silent night, holy night . . ."

And suddenly something in the poignant scene—a boy was pushing his toy car down long avenues of the dead—put me back in another life. I had come to Bolivia before, twenty-six years before, as a teenager, just released from high school, with a classmate; for three months we had bumped across Central and South America on buses, taking in the tough and unaccountable world that school had trained us for. When, a quarter of a century later, the trip came back to me, it was only Bolivia, of all the nine countries we'd visited, that kept bobbing up: the bowler-hatted women laboring up the steep streets near the cathedral, unsold goods slung over their shoulders; the billowing, snow-white clouds that looked fantastical in skies as sharp as those of Lhasa; the square-headed statues in the Altiplano, barely excavated in centuries.

Around me in the crystal, breathless air, which gave to everything a sense of excitement, I'd seen sorcerers with many-colored woolen earflaps, muttering incantations as they sat on the ground outside the cathedral; others were waving sticks at the villagers who came to them in search of charms and spells. This was the country that sat in the *Guinness Book of World Records* for the most changes of government (in other words, coups d'état) per annum; this was the city where Cervantes himself, father of Quixote and a former convict, had once applied to become mayor (and failed).

I always loved being alone—I had grown up commuting on planes between my parents' home in California and my schools in England—and so long as I was loose in the world, uncompanioned, I was never bored or at a loss. Freed from my usual routine and small talk, I was away from the sense that I had to play a role, or to choose one self over another; I could find what lay at the heart of me, my core, and so bring back something clearer and more rounded to the people I loved. Home, I began to feel, was the half-formed beliefs you fashioned in the middle of all you didn't and couldn't understand, a tent on a wide, empty plain.

Now, as I got ready to step out of the Plaza Hotel, to go to Titicaca, I called up my mother, in India with family for the holidays, and my sweetheart of fourteen years, Hiroko, celebrating the New Year in Japan, to wish them a good year; I'd see them both in a few days, as soon as my immersion in this other world was over. I looked to the street, where soldiers were pointing out the Three Wise Men—on llamas—to their toddlers, and then headed out myself, up the Prado, towards the area of magicians, to find a travel agency that could convey me across the Altiplano.

Taxis with "Droopy" on the top juddered past on the Himalayan slopes, and before long I was stepping into a bus to travel across the Andean plateau. The Altiplano is as desolate and humbling an area as I have seen; figures in the distance are reduced to specks and all that is really visible are the huge shadows the sun casts across the mountains. It's not hard to feel as if you're entering the realm of parable, with humans just disposable tokens in a much grander drama of changelessness and change.

As the bus, groaning and faltering, began to sputter out of town, the other great presence of my life came back to me again. It had been a mild October day—I was at college—and my girlfriend of the time and I had seen my father unexpectedly walking across the courtyard to our room. As in some bedroom farce, Kristin had slithered out of a back window—she was the incarnation, as we both knew, of every parent's worst fears—while I prepared myself for the sudden visitation. My college had been my father's college, too, and I guessed he had just flown over from California to England, on his way to an annual Club of Rome meeting to discuss the future of mankind.

As soon as I heard his knock, I opened up, to see him in his regular gear: black corduroy jacket, dark slacks, an overcoat against the early autumn chill and a blazing yellow shirt. What he saw—it struck me now—would be a skinny teenager with hair made (the boy hoped) for a lead guitarist, and lots of high-toned European novels more made to impress than really to enlighten.

As he walked into the room, my father might have been walking into his own vanished youth, twenty-six years before; he had arrived from Bombay and been given a prize room in the ancient cloisters (so cold to a newcomer from the tropics that he'd requested to be moved to somewhere less full of history). Now, as he looked at me, he started talking about the French poet Jean Cocteau.

Once, he said—had he seen or only heard this?—Cocteau had dashed off a sketch of a human figure. The result was so spooky—evil, to be honest—that just to put it on the wall was to curse the room forever, so it seemed.

Why was he telling me this, I asked myself? What did it have to do with anything? It was only decades later that I realized that perhaps, like any father, he was trying to protect his dangerously unworldly only child from all the sides of life the boy was so sure he knew everything about. Or warning him against the easy ways he might try to forge his own destiny. When my father came back to spend a full term in the town, eighteen months later, Kristin, warm and solicitous for all her demons, was the one (as in every other Greene novel) to keep him company over dinner and to make sure that everything in his apartment was okay

Now, as we passed across the emptiness of the dry brown plain in Bolivia, I noticed a woman near the front of the bus stealing glances at me. She was in her late thirties, I guessed, with many of her youthful dreams exhausted, but she hadn't given up on her earliest hopes entirely. She had applied some lipstick and blusher this morning and put on a cross that silvered her throat; she seemed to be trying to work out who I was as I sat in my row alone, looking out on the sand-colored quiet.

Finally, as we drew near Copacabana, she struggled back through the jouncing vehicle and asked me if I was the person who had requested a guide. I was, so she sat down beside me and, pulling her shoulder-length hair back from her face, smiled and began to tell me the facts of Bolivia in a spirited near-English.

Whatever was really compelling here, though, lay outside

the reach of facts and figures: a brown-hooded Catholic priest was standing outside the main church as we drew into town, blessing the toy cars and houses that villagers had brought to him. Some of the indigenous souls before him were carrying dolls swaddled in blankets, and he was making the sign of the cross above them and above some SUVs. This was the leap of faith I had seen, in both directions, on every continent: the Indians would believe that this figure could stand for something greater—as wide as the high skies above them—regardless of the man he was in private; he, in turn, would leave his usual self behind to try to extend some blessing to these strangers. My guide looked up at me, and I asked her how much these people were Christian, how much listening to some older law.

She couldn't say exactly—or didn't want to—and when we got off the bus, I suggested she take a couple of hours off, so she could be free of me and the recitation of numbers; when we met up again in early afternoon, she broke into a warm smile as if we were long-lost friends. We got into a boat and traveled out to a sunlit island—the Capri of Lake Titicaca, it could seem—and climbed up a hill to look down upon the water. "This is a place to escape to," she said, and something wistful came into the midsummer day. Maybe this was not only a job for her, but an excursion, a way to step into another life?

On the boat back into town, she started to rub the stress out of my shoulders. "Too much reading," she said, with a shy smile. "Too much writing."

Night was beginning to fall as we got into the bus for the long trip back. Most of the other passengers were falling asleep where they sat, and in any case we were curtained off from them by the foreign language we spoke. The seats were small, so we were very close. As she asked me about my life in Japan, I could see all the glimmering lights—freedom, mobility, the lure of the far-off—that had come into the friendly woman's life this day. I'd found this theme echoed in every page of Graham Greene: the foreigner, precisely by going to another country, brings a whiff of a different world into the lives of the locals he meets. From that point on, both are in the shadowland that lies between the existence we lead and the one we occasionally dream of.

"It's strange to have lost my passport today," I said, as occasional lamps from passing huts flickered behind us in the dark. "It's almost like losing my identity."

We'd come to a small lake that morning and stepped into a rowboat to go across it. When we'd emerged at the other shore, two policemen in uniforms had asked us for IDs. I'd presented a passport (a backup one I carried for just such moments), and they'd looked at it, looked at me and then taken the passport away. I never saw it again.

"Of course!" my guide had said, with a laugh. "The last foreign people who came here who looked like you were hiding in La Paz while they prepared their attack on New York City. Why else would someone from a poor country come to Bolivia?"

Now, as we remembered the moment, the woman laughed again and put a hand on my arm. A local habit, I thought; but perhaps not only a local habit. I could see her smile in the dark—it was pitch black outside as we lurched through the emptiness—and a part of me wondered what she was smiling at, or for. My life was as hazy to her as hers might be to me; each of us could fill in the empty space with anything we chose.

In Graham Greene books such equivocal partnerships may be all that we can hope for; in a world where there are no absolutes, a qualified friendship based on your lack of illusions in the other (and in yourself) may be the only thing you can trust. In life, however, I'm not sure how much anyone is really happy on such uncertain ground; this woman had two children, whom this day was supporting, and I had a wife, Hiroko, in Japan. As we began to inch through the jam-packed streets not far from El Alto—the huge slum that marked the fastest growing city in South America—I passed on my hopes for her children's future and, a little guiltily (I was never good at telling people what they needed to hear), warm thanks for all her guidance. Hastily, stumbling a little as she stood up—was it embarrassment? or only disappointment?—she rose to her feet in the narrow aisle and I pressed some notes in her palm, saying there was no need for her to come all the way to my hotel, I could find my way back there alone.

She fumbled her way through the bus and as it pulled away, she waved from the crowded sidewalk, in the dark, and then became just another face in the crowd, turning around to walk down the almost black, unpaved alleyways that led to corrugated-iron shacks, mountains of trash rising by their sides.

∴

Graham Greene is often taken to be the patron saint of the foreigner alone, drifting between certainties; his territory is the small apartment in the very foreign town, the passion that is temporary, the border crossing that seems the perfect home for the man who prays to a God he's not sure he believes in. In the last twenty-seven years of his life he inhabited a simply furnished two-room apartment above the port in Antibes, in France, not far from Monaco, and shared his afternoons (though not his nights) with Yvonne Cloetta, the longtime companion who remained married throughout their affair. Though he was technically married for sixty-five years, he spent the last forty-three of them alone.

If you try to push him into a compartment, you'll always get it a little wrong. Call him a "Catholic novelist," as many did, and you'll be reminded that he liked to call himself a "Catholic agnostic" and stressed, as the years went on, that he had faith but not belief (the emotional but not the rational basis for religion). Note how many of his novels are set along what were in his lifetime the shabby, forgotten margins of the world—Havana, Saigon, the Belgian Congo, West Africa—and you have to concede that those foreign places and their people are mostly backdrops for a much more personal, exacting enquiry into states of being—goodness, peace, involvement—he longed for but could never quite find. Point out how English he is, and you have to acknowledge that Englishness is precisely what he's trying to get away from.

A lonely man, finding himself in a turbulent place he doesn't know quite what to do with—this is how his later fables begin, usually—takes on a pretty, young local companion; she gives him calm and kindness, but her very sweetness reminds him of how unworthy he is, and his sense of protectiveness makes him want to defend her even from himself. The tangled politics of the scene ensure that he has no shortage of enemies, though generally he has one good friend—another foreigner—whose very vulnerability intensifies the protagonist's sense of unease. God hovers everywhere around the scene, but usually, like many a love, He is known only by His refusal to do what we most want.

In Greene's archetypal novel, *The Quiet American,* a middle-aged Englishman, Fowler, lives in Saigon during the last days of French rule there, with a twenty-year-old Vietnamese woman, Phuong, whom he's met at the Grand Monde dance hall. As soon as a young American, Pyle, appears on the scene, Fowler senses that he is going to be displaced by this fresh and dangerously innocent new power. As his country will be displaced by America. When the young arrival, a picture of his parents on his desk, turns his chivalrous attention on Phuong, Fowler finds new reason to resent him— especially because the quiet American is clearly a more gallant and unstained, a more openly tender suitor than any jaded Englishman can be.

After Pyle saves his life, Fowler feels more beholden (and therefore hostile) to him than ever. (Greene would always be shrewd enough to see that few of us can forgive a good deed done to us—God's law and man's seldom converge—and, as he puts it in the book, we can never be betrayed by an enemy, only by a friend.) Completed in 1955, the novel tells the story of Britain feeling its empire slipping away and trying to protect itself from hurt by claiming not to care. It tells the story (which is to say, the future) of young America coming to the older cultures of the world and determined to remake them with the latest ideas of Harvard Yard. And it tells the story of a supple and responsive Asia that, precisely by gauging the needs of every foreign visitor, and giving each back a reflection of his desires, will always remain on top of them, or at least outside their grasp.

Yet on a more intimate level, it pierces much more deeply.

We can feel the barely suppressed romanticism of the English-man, who cannot admit even to himself how much he's lost himself to the foreign land that has softened him and to the young woman who offers what he hungers for most poignantly, peace. We are stung by the young American's unpreparedness for a world he is determined to rescue, whether it's in need of rescue or not. And we can see how the Vietnamese in the middle, drawing on centuries of silent tradition, manages her destiny by putting pragmatism before emotion; romance and reality change places with every scene.

"When I first came," Fowler confesses of his time in Viet-nam, "I counted the days of my assignment, like a schoolboy marking off the days of term." Now he's turned in the other direction and searches for ways of avoiding a return to any-where he might think of as home. A schoolboy still, perhaps, in a decidedly complex version of Abroad, but alive so long as he's surrounded by people, a culture, a faith he can't get to the bottom of.

CHAPTER 2

Who are these figures who take residence inside our heads, to the point where we can feel them shivering inside us even when we want to "be ourselves"? Who put them there, and why this man I've never met, and not that one? If I were to choose a secret companion, an unofficial alter ego, I would most likely fasten on someone more dashing, more decisive, less unsettled than Greene; if Providence were choosing one, it might alight on someone who lived in the same high-school building as I, attended the same university, traveled around the Far East, as I did when young, visited the university where my parents were teaching and then watched his house in the California hills burn down, as I had done—someone like Aldous Huxley. But our shadow associates are, like parents (or godparents), presences we've never chosen and, like many of our loves or compulsions, blur the lines inside us by living beyond our explanations.

They make as little sense as the gods we choose to believe in, or the devils. Graham Greene could never be a fantasy figure for me, like the smooth secret agents whose adventures we devoured in our wood-creaking rooms at the Dragon School in Oxford, or the Lakers shooting guard whose poster I put up on my wall in high school, near London, to mock the copy of *Agamemnon* on my desk. He was never a writer I dreamed of becoming, a wise man on top of things. If anything, as the product of the England where I grew up, he was part of all that I was trying to put behind me; he belonged with the hesitant stutter of the radiator in the red-brick classroom, the low grey skies and weathered walls that put us in our place and kept us there; he was the kind of writer teachers would urge us to pick up in the holidays, or enlist in their cunning gambits as they handed out this term's divinity textbook, shrewdly called *Guard Thou Our Disbelief.*

"Always, everywhere, there is some voice crying from a tower," he'd written in *The Quiet American*—it was all but the heart of his doctrine and his work—and as soon as one voice is answered, there is another, then another, and that one may be inside of us. That wasn't what we wanted to hear at all.

∴

But there he is, in spite of everything. Not a hero or a counselor or the kind of person I would otherwise want to claim as kin. I see the gangly, long-legged figure graciously receiving a visitor in his room and keeping the intruder at bay with an offer of a drink, folding his awkward limbs around himself on the sofa; I see the high color in his cheeks, and the pale, unearthly blue eyes that speak to everyone of the troubled depths he's both concealing and perceiving in the world. He talks in a slightly strangled English voice, surprisingly thin and reedy, and, when amused, he breaks into an unhardened, high-pitched giggle, suddenly, that equally abruptly stops, as if he's been caught out, the mischievous boy escaping, for a moment, from the sharp-eyed keeper of his own counsel. "A precocious schoolboy," his friend Lady Read noted once, "with tremendous depths . . . and these are the depths one doesn't enquire into."

I remember walking into a long-distance telephone parlor in the sleepy Mexican town of Mérida one hot August afternoon. I was with Hiroko, sharing with her the pyramids nearby, and we needed to make a call back to Japan. In 1996 telephones weren't easy to come by in such places, and we knew a call from our hotel room would deliver us instantly into static, or possible bankruptcy at the same time.

We wandered down the main street after lunch, away from the main plaza, strolling along the side of the road where there was shade, past cafés and little tourist shops, brightly colored piñatas and swinging donkeys, and came at last upon a little travel agency that advertised "International Calls." Just like the places in California where Mexicans call back home, though here it was we who were the petitioners, and the ones who could barely speak the language. We went in and saw three little wooden booths—confessionals, in effect—and, in front of them, a counter and a young Mexican woman.

In fumbled Spanish I told her that we wanted to place a call to Japan and, nodding, she began completing, very slowly, a request form on a pad of paper. As she did so, a man came out from the back—the boss—and, to my surprise, I saw that he was from India, surely the only person of Indian descent other than myself in this provincial Yucatán town. Perhaps he had seen me through a spyhole and wanted to satisfy his curiosity, as now I did mine? Perhaps he was simply eager, as I was, to find someone to speak English to? In either case, I might, at some level, have been looking at a reflection of myself, in this unlikely soul, in his thirties, alert and clearly inquisitive, who had chosen to live in a forgotten foreign place far from the obvious sustenance of home.

How had he gotten here? How long had he been here? Who else was with him? My questions began to multiply and he, perhaps grateful for some company, began to ask me similar questions in return. I didn't quite elucidate that I lived in a tiny neighborhood in rural Japan, with Hiroko, thousands of miles from the nearest relative, in a land where officials were inclined to strip-search me every other time I entered, so improbable did my presence seem. I didn't quite say that a physical location is unimportant so long as you live among values and assumptions that strike you as your own—or the ones you'd like to learn. I didn't even go so far as to assert that home lies in the things you carry with you everywhere and not the ones that tie you down. I noticed him putting a hand on the girl's arm, and so another question was answered, and a life began to form behind the counter.

Why Mexico? Why not the Gulf States or East Africa, or even Kobe, in Japan, where there would be other Indians like himself to share the burden of displacement? My ancestral people are an itinerant lot, given to putting themselves in far-away places where the law of supply and demand will sustain them even if that of cause and effect does not; in the battered Alaskan town of Skagway, a few years later, I'd run into a man from Bombay, with his wife and daughter, draping golden necklaces and pendants over the hands of cruise-ship passengers, in a tiny Gold Rush settlement that for seven months of every year saw no visitors at all. In Alice Springs sixteen months on, the man who checked me in to my hotel during a sudden downpour in the desert was a friendly émigré from Bombay, another Bombay exile smiling behind the counter of the next hotel down the street.

But this man was alone, in terms of obvious kin, and I wondered about his nights, whom he turned to in the dark. Hiroko and I walked back to our hotel in the hot afternoon—knowing we'd be away tomorrow, in the next town of exiles—and yet I never really left the man behind. When I got back to Japan, I wrote a story imagining his life and now, more than fifteen years later, I'm still thinking about him, much more than I think about the ruins at Palenque or the see-through green waters running along the beach at Cancún.

Other writers had offered me a version of the man, in similar places, but no one had found him so persistently in every corner of the globe as Greene had. I remembered, long after returning from Mérida, that Greene, in his nonfictional account of a trip across Mexico in 1937, *The Lawless Roads*, had, everywhere he turned, found Germans curiously settled in the middle of a forbidding landscape, solitary Americans riding the trains, people who ended up in an alien and sometimes terrifying country as if in some haunted place within themselves. "I wondered what odd whim of Providence had landed him here," he had written of a German, "a teacher of languages in a Mexican mining town." I didn't remember then—or know—that Greene had written once about a stranger from India he came across when he was twenty-one. "He stayed in my mind—a symbol of the shabby, the inefficient and possibly the illegal." I might, again, have been walking through a plot he'd dreamed up years before.

∴

It is often night in Greene's fiction, and the scene usually turns around those two men together. They're in a foreign place and circumstances are treacherous. They've nurtured all kinds of unflattering impressions of each other and, in a simpler world, they'd always remain apart, safe in their sense of enmity.

But—in *The Quiet American,* say—Fowler and Pyle find themselves in a lonely watchtower above the rice paddies of the Vietnamese countryside after night has fallen, and two young local soldiers cower in the same space. Mines and gunfire explode outside as the evening deepens and somehow, brought closer by their sense of danger and the need for companionship, the two foreigners begin to talk of God and death, the women they have and haven't loved. Each ministers to the other, just by listening, and honesty and intensity rise quickly as neither knows if he'll make it through the night.

The scenes rarely turn around a man and a woman and, in any case, men and women are seldom able to understand each other fully in Greene; they don't share the same anxieties or fears. And there are seldom group scenes in Greene, rarely more than three or four people in a room. You realize quickly that friendship is his theme, more than romance; he became famous for traveling with loyal friends—the priest Leopoldo Duran, the journalist Bernard Diederich, the Hollywood producer Alexander Korda (whose movies he'd savaged as a critic)—and friendship seemed a kind of sacrament for him because with friends (unlike with loves) we don't have agendas or designs. You can't read the books in terms of ideologies, because both circumstances and the heart are so contradictory that no one who is honest can ever settle to anything for long; even the man of faith—maybe especially he—lives most of the time with doubt. You can't read the books in terms of "gender issues" or colonialism, because in the dark all distinctions disappear, and we're reduced to something essential and often scared.

Greene seldom even tried to portray a native of the countries he described (let alone a young female character); his theme was foreignness, displacedness. And he kept on coming back to innocence, chivalry, as if he could not forgive them for so often leading to disenchantment in the end. Yet every assumption he sets up in us is overturned by each new twist in his painfully intricate plots.

At the end of *The Quiet American,* Fowler, already jittery, runs into the loud journalist who was "an emblematic statue of all I thought I hated in America." Throughout the book Granger has seemed coarse, cynical and domineering (and we can tell that Greene thought of himself as a journalist because journalists are almost the only group he treats disimissively in his fiction). When he sees this loud American coming up to him, the Englishman braces for a fight. But the man he likes to look down upon addresses him directly. I need to talk to you, Granger says; it's my son's eighth birthday, and he has polio, and things are looking bad. You don't like me and "you think you know everything," but you're the only one I have to talk to here.

Fowler tries to help—he learns that Granger has been praying, though he doesn't really have faith—but now he is less able than ever to settle to anything. The man isn't a buffoon, he sees; just a soul in pain. "Perhaps in Paradise," Greene wrote in a private notebook, "we are given the power to help the living. I picture Paradise as a place of activity." In Greene it's rarely our actions that get us into trouble, so much as our uncertain thoughts.

∴

I was in Saigon one autumn, and had just checked in to the Hotel Majestic, along the Saigon River. It was midnight— which meant ten in the morning in California, where I'd woken up—and the day (for me) was just beginning. I walked along Dong Khoi Street (formerly Tu Do, or "Freedom," Street) towards the Hotel Continental, a central site in *The Quiet American.* As I did so, I wondered how much places, or people, ever really change. They adopt new fashions with the seasons, lose hair or see crows' feet gather around their eyes; yet the girl who was once nine years old is still visible in the grandmother of eighty-four.

Dong Khoi (or "Simultaneous Uprising") Street was alive with the somewhat illicit energy I recalled from an earlier trip, thirteen years before. The sound of "Layla" drifted up from an underground bar, and when I looked in on another '60s-themed place—the Jefferson Airplane were playing "White Rabbit"—I saw Japanese couples shyly sipping at "Lynchburg Lemonades" and "Girls Scout Cookies." Men in the shadows whispered promises of exotic pleasures and *cyclo* drivers pedaled slowly past, sometimes with a young woman in their throne, sometimes stopping to ask me if I wanted a friend for the night.

As I made my way down the street—"Massage, massage," murmured the men who were standing around—a young woman on a motorbike suddenly veered in front of me, stopped and, taking off her helmet, shook free her long hair.

"We go my room?" she asked.

The French war, the American war, the war against the Khmer Rouge had all come and gone, yet Saigon seemed not so different from what Greene had seen in 1951. Alive with adrenaline energy and the excitement of arrival—free at last after twenty hours in a plane—I stepped into an Internet café to try to catch the scene while it was still alive within me.

"It's eerie," I wrote to a friend who had grown up in the same neighborhood when I was six years old (his father had been a colleague of my own, teaching political philosophy at Oxford). "Phuong and Fowler, out from their room on the Rue Catinat, are all around me. I can almost imagine Greene, raincoat buttoned tightly around his throat, slipping around the next corner. It's like stepping into his Vietnam novel."

My friend, like so many of the boys I'd grown up with, had become a traveler and a novelist in a deeply Greenian mode, spinning out stories of Englishmen of the middle classes, far from home and being tugged away from their lives by foreign affairs, uneasy questions, the streets of Panama. These stories, of lonely and displaced civil servants, or outsiders caught up in civil wars, might almost have constituted an entire genre, post-Greene; I sometimes thought that that was what school trained us for—Empire in the post-imperial age, toughing it out abroad and living in spartan places by ourselves, learning to observe, to read the world, to play at being unofficial spies. I recalled how, on my last trip here, when I'd gone to the "Continental Shelf" in search of local intelligence, I'd met a former colleague of sorts from *Time* magazine who had revealed, at war's end, that he had been a North Vietnamese colonel all along, one of the "enemy's" best sources of information. Now he sat among returning reporters, asking wistful questions about California.

As I tapped away at my excited account, trying to inhale the smells and ironies to send across the waters to England (or New Mexico, or wherever my friend happened to be), a woman slipped in from the N.Y.-Saigon bar next door.

Greene would never have called her a woman; she was a girl, as confounding as any of her cousins who attach themselves to foreign males abroad, with a beauty-queen face and a tigress air to her and, I was sure, a keen head for numbers. She was tiny and wearing high heels, and her legs were long and shapely.

Business must be slow in the N.Y.-Saigon today, I thought as she perched herself on one of the tall stools in front of a terminal and began logging on to her hotmail account.

If you have a dangerous curiosity about the world, or if you're just a writer of sorts, trained to collect observations, you become, in such situations, shameless. "There is a splinter of ice," Greene wrote in his memoir, "in the heart of a writer," and he needs that sense of cool remove to do his job, as any diagnostician does. I looked over, while deep in my message, to see what the young lady was responding to.

It was (of course) a love letter from an admirer now in Germany. "Dear Phuong," it began, and the immemorial cadences of half-requited love tumbled out.

"You know," I could imagine my friend Henry saying, "Greene stayed in the Majestic, too." (I hadn't known.) "That was where he met the young women whom he turned into Phuong."

∴

O f course, Greene might have said, if presented with such evidence; a writer's job is to see what will happen to a stranger tomorrow. He has to plunge so deeply into his recesses that he touches off tremors that find an echo in a reader; and if he goes deep enough into the subconscious, he will find the future hidden there as much as the past. A writer is a palmist, reading the lines of the planet.

Greene never wanted to be seen as fortune-teller or prophet, but I'd found him leading as much as shadowing me across the globe, if only because he listened to the world so closely he knew what it would do next, as any of us might do with an old friend or love. Were I to go to Cuba tomorrow, the only guidebook I'd take, to lead me through its animated torpor and the lightning passions that make it at once so alluring and so confounding, would be his portrait of pre-Revolutionary Havana in 1958. When I visited the Hotel Oloffson in Port-au-Prince, thirty-six years after Greene's *Comedians*, it was to find, to the syllable, the ghostly hotel that he'd described (still, as in his book, with but one guest in residence). At the cocktail hour, a slippery charmer called Aubelin Joliecoeur (gossip columnist and seeming government informer) drifted into the lobby, looking for new friends and eager to gather data on all the newcomers off the plane. To many he would say, "You've met me already in the work of my friend, Monsieur Grin. Petit Pierre in *The Comedians*."

Ten years before American involvement in Vietnam approached its peak, Greene was writing about "napalm bombings" and describing CIA intrigue there and fumbled attempts to make contact with local proxies. The whole of *The Quiet American* could be taken as a questioning of men's efforts to save a world that's much larger than their ideas: "God save us always from the innocent and the good," Fowler says early on, with typical (if slightly showy) Greenian irony; half a novel later, he tells the quiet American, "I wish sometimes you had a few bad motives, you might understand a little more about human beings."

Yet even as he's outlining, enduringly, the perils of high- and simple-minded innocence around the world, Greene is also, more subtly, stripping the veil from the Englishman, so keen to tell us that he's not involved, if only to persuade himself that he's too seasoned to have feelings or opinions. Even the young American can see through him. "Now you are pretending to be tough, Thomas," he says to the English Fowler and, sixteen pages later, "I guess you're just trying to be tough. There's something you must believe in" (and there is, we see—in the prospect of peace, the hope of a temporary permanence with his Vietnamese girl, a life abroad, all the things Fowler keeps telling himself he doesn't care about). *The Quiet American* is still cited, and not only in Hanoi, as a timeless look at the vagaries of American foreign policy, but inside it hides a more private and anguished book, much deeper, that could be called *The Unquiet Englishman.* The words that recur, again and again, in its opening pages are "pain" and "love" and "innocence" and "home," and it's not always easy to tell one from the other.

I looked back at the real Phuong now, typing out an answer to her faraway suitor in Europe. "I think about you all the time," I knew she'd write, though misspelling a few of the words. "I miss you. When you come back Saigon?"

Then she noticed I was spying on her and gave me a long, slow smile, an invitation. I could be her Fowler tonight, she might have been saying—or her Pyle. A watchful English-born journalist or a naïve young graduate from the New World, so eager to save her and her country that he seemed certain to ensure the destruction of them both. I knew about such girls because I'd met them in the movie of Greene's *Honorary Consul,* viewed many times just before I took off for Southeast Asia at the age of twenty-six. On arrival in the tropics I'd found precisely the mix of languor and alertness, apparent complaisance and self-possession that Phuong embodies in all the professional charmers who'd been so keen to be my (or any visiting foreigner's) friend.

The problem was, they were never so simple as my notions of them. They were much sweeter and more open and unguarded than their profession would suggest—and never quite so innocent or dreamy as they professionally suggested. They were—as Phuong is—walking paradoxes of a kind, deliberately blurring the gap between material and emotional need, more impenetrable even than those British and American men who were busily rearranging their names and selves so as to respond to the flattering attentions of young beauties.

Greene loved to write and talk of brothels, paid companions, and it was one of the habits that put off many an otherwise sympathetic reader, or convinced friends that they were dealing with an adolescent. But underneath the wished-for bravado there always seemed to lie something quieter and more sincere than simply a wish to shock. He really did appear to hold that kindness is more important than conventional morality and the things we do more telling than merely the things we claim to believe. In one play that he barely acknowledged—it was never published in his lifetime—he portrays the girls in a whorehouse as earthly angels of a kind, listening to men's confessions and offering a form of absolution, as elsewhere priests might do.

The only crime in such a place, he suggests—the play is called A *House of Reputation*—is to feel shame about one's presence there (as a dentist does) or to complicate the exchange with talk of love (as one "sentimental ignorant fool" does, falling for a hardheaded girl as if he's confusing the woman with her office). When the boy in love gets the brothel closed down, in a fit of too-simple righteousness, he strips the girl he loves of her home and her living and deprives the world of a much-needed hospital of the heart. The only sins in the Greene universe are hypocrisy and putting a theory—even a religion—before a human being.

CHAPTER 3

Phuong means "phoenix," the author tells us on the opening page of *The Quiet American;* it stands for something that rises again and again from the ashes, whether those of warfare or of love. It stands for a country, you could say, that is still standing, and bustling about its business, even after being attacked by France and then by the United States, while having China on its doorstep; it stands for a spirit that never dies, too, and perhaps a figure—a situation, a setting—that arises again and again even as the rue Catinat becomes raucous Tu Do Street, and then "Simultaneous Uprising" Street. Phuong steps out of the milk bar and back into the road, to meet her aging English suitor, and a generation or two later another sylphlike beauty appears along a dark street in Saigon, after midnight, and tries to entice a newcomer in the terms of her new century.

I went back to the Majestic—girls around the lobby gazed hopefully up at me—and tried to pick up the thread of my own life. Walking through a book by an author long dead is not a comforting experience; I began to feel I was just a compound ghost that someone else had dreamed up, and his novels were my unwritten autobiography. I had reread *The Quiet American* perhaps seven times at that point, sometimes feeling my sympathies with the Englishman, whom I recalled from friends at school, sometimes with the young American (whom I had met when studying innocence in Harvard Yard). Sometimes I even felt my heart with the Asian woman, whose wise acceptances and gift for adapting to any situation were a large part of what I hoped to learn when bringing myself back to my parents' continent.

Yet if I were really to want to learn about hauntedness— those people who seem so to stalk our footsteps that we can never be sure if they have slipped inside our beings or we are just drifting through their imaginations—the writer I would most likely turn to is, in fact, Graham Greene. The dream analyst he lived with as a boy no doubt reminded him that it was his mother's first cousin who gave the world the story of Dr. Jekyll and Mr. Hyde, the perfect image for a writer who would habitually describe himself, like his grandfather, as manic-depressive, unable in his melancholy moods to imagine the prankster who, when full of deranged energy, could not begin to imagine that person who felt leaden, weighed down with guilt. Greene ends his slippery memoir, *Ways of Escape*— ways of escaping telling us anything at all, a skeptical reader might say—with an enigmatic epilogue called "The Other," in which he describes how relentlessly shadowed he had long been by a man (or maybe two) who traveled the world, seeming to slip into his identity and doing the wildest things in his name.

He received letters from strangers he'd never met, the novelist Greene tells us, that fondly remembered times they had passed together; he saw photographs in newspapers, from Jamaica to Geneva, of "Graham Greene the writer" squiring glamorous women around town and looking debonair (though the women in the photos were as strange to him as the man posing as "Graham Greene the writer," who used his name to stay on tea plantations and wrote letters to an English magazine, claiming to be "simply a newsman after the truth").

At one point, the "other" Graham Greene seemed to end up in jail and asked the *Picture Post* in London to send him a hundred pounds because he'd lost his passport; it did so, and when the real Greene was tracked down, he promptly suggested to the same magazine that he fly over to Assam to interview his alter ego. Before long, however, the nimble impersonator had skipped bail and was off to his next exotic destination, or the next woman he planned to charm, partly by saying he was Graham Greene.

It might almost have been a parable Greene had fashioned about the paradoxes of writing: the man who bares a part of his soul on the page soon finds that his friends are treating him as strangers, bewildered by this other self they've met in his book. Meanwhile, many a stranger is considering him a friend, convinced he knows this man he's read, even if he's never met him. The paradox of reading is that you draw closer, to some other creature's voice within you than to the people who surround you (with their surfaces) every day.

Greene had long been fascinated, he confessed, by a poem of Edward Thomas's, "The Other," about a man shadowing someone like himself—"I pursued / To prove the likeness, and, if true, / To watch until myself I knew"—and now he wondered if, in following the exploits of this fugitive, he was indeed learning something about himself. Once, after having lunch with President Allende in Chile, he was himself taken to be the "unreal" Graham Greene, a fake. "Had I been the impostor all the time?" he ends his memoirs by writing. "Was I the Other?"

Yet Greene was never quite so innocent as he claimed; he had devised an Other of his own, whom he called "Hilary Tench," and sometimes he would address his wife or win magazine competitions under the pseudonym of "H. Tench," a dark and cruel figure who seemed to speak for a shadow self, the unconscious impulses that made him do things "unlike himself" that he wished belonged to someone else. Traveling, he gave out business cards with the names of characters from his books on them, among them "H. Tench," and the first two words in his most celebrated novel, *The Power and the Glory*, are "Mr. Tench," the name he gives an exiled dentist who lives in a Mexican village. Greene sometimes kept two versions of his diary—the book in which he might be expected to be most transparent—as if there were at least two versions of any day or story, Jekyll's, perhaps, and Hyde's.

One day, he found another "Graham Greene" listed in the London phone book—the name is common enough—and called up the poor man to ask if he was the one responsible for the "filthy novels." When the man stammered out his demurral—yes, his name was Graham Greene, but he was a retired solicitor—Greene berated him further for not having the courage to confess to the scandalous writings.

It was a curious kind of self-attack from a man who claimed to have been assaulted (or praised) by strangers for deeds he had never committed; it spoke to a theological vision that suggested that few of us are innocents, yet all of us are innocent of most of the crimes that we are accused of, often by ourselves.

Slipping in and out of identities would be what kept Greene alive, officially and otherwise, all his life.

∴

Graham Greene the novelist appeals to some of us, I think—even challenges our sense of who we are—in part because he is so acutely sensitive to all the ways we can fail to understand one another, even those people closest to ourselves; he knew his characters, he wrote in his memoirs, better than he knew anyone in real life. He becomes the caretaker of that part of us that feels that we are larger and much harder to contain than even we can get our heads around, and that there is a mystery, fundamental and unanswerable, in ourselves as in the world around us, which is in fact a part of what gives life its sense of hauntedness. It's the best side of us, in his books—our conscience, our sense of sympathy, our feeling for another's pain—that causes us the deepest grief. And God, if He even exists, is less a source of solace than a hound of Heaven, always on our path.

Graham Greene knew the craving for knowledge, the horror of being reductively known that seems to trouble some of us. He inscribed his copy of *The Quiet American* in French to Yvonne, his companion of more than thirty years, "From the unknown Graham." He knew that some things make little sense, like the fact that a con man can impersonate one of the best-known writers in the world, or that a scruffy mongrel living in Japan can feel that his deepest life story is being told by an Englishman of two generations before. The haunting power of his novels, often, comes from the "hunted man" at their center, the fugitive whom we long to see to safety as he tries to flee his pursuers and find the stillness and comfort that are all we can expect of Heaven (and are equally far from our reach). The pathos, the smothered kindness of his novels comes from the fact that the more generously the man tries to act, the more remote his salvation seems to become.

∴

When I was a boy, a terrible chill went through me as soon as I heard the opening chords, and voice-over, of the television show in the next room, where my parents sat at night. Television was a new presence then, especially in Oxford, a disembodied voice suddenly in our midst, and I could not begin to understand why the words so terrified me. But every time I heard the theme song of *The Fugitive* and the opening sentences about a wrongly convicted doctor in pursuit of a one-armed man who has killed the doctor's wife, some ancient terror rose up and I buried myself more deeply under my bedclothes, trying to block out the sound, though now the image of a man running, out of breath, across the black-and-white darkness, and a killer on the loose, was with me all night, as potent as any memory of the convict Magwitch suddenly rising from among the gravestones in *Great Expectations*.

Childhood is the time when such terrors are alive in us, unnameable but devouring, as if we are just back from a realm where a penetrating darkness is as present to us as an unfallen Eden, and we cannot put away the memory of either. The space at the back of our garden, which I never went close to, because I was sure that to go there was to lose myself, to be sucked into a black hole forever; the name of the children's home that I would sometimes hear my parents mention, as the place where I might end up if I misbehaved; the tread of my friends' father as he came up the stairs after lights-out, wielding a shoe he was ready to use on any one of us: all of them haunt me still, as very little in my subsequent life has the power to.

Like any little boy, I was terrified of the masked man who loomed down on me, wielding silver drills and sticks to poke into my mouth, assuring me, "This won't hurt," because he knew it would. The implements lined up beside the basin were instruments of torture. My mother took me along at regular intervals to the dentist on Beaumont Street, in Oxford, and, as a good local boy drinking nonfluoridated water and eating sugar-filled toffees for every other meal, I always had several holes in my mouth that the dentist was eager to probe and prick and explore.

Dentists are a constant preoccupation in Greene, the most chilling image in daily life of a faceless administer of justice; you can find them everywhere in his world (even in Mexico, the local man who accompanies a nonfictional Greene to a nightclub, and then the vocal American he encounters on a boat, are dentists. In the little town of Orizaba, he sees "a whole street of dentists' shops"; dentists come to speak for the way pain and its seeming cure, our powerlessness and our ter- rifying redemption, lie all about us). A dentist is really a priest in a different kind of white robe, administering suffering as a way, he assures us, of keeping deeper suffering at bay.

I didn't know, as I walked, aged five or six, to Beaumont Street that, only a few doors away, Mrs. Graham Greene had recently made her home, with the novelist's two children, scratching into a window with her diamond ring her and her husband's initials next to the dates of every time he chose to revisit her. I had no reason to be aware that Graham Greene himself had lived for a time off the Woodstock Road, five minutes away by foot, the road on which I was born (in the same hospital as his daughter), and next to the road on which I grew up. I learned only long after beginning this book that Greene's son went to the same elementary school that I did, the Dragon, down the street.

∴

My closest friend when I was at school was a fresh-faced son of privilege who was so deeply rooted in the ruling classes of England that he clearly longed for everything that was the opposite: escape, at least for a while. We sat in our dusty medieval classroom, while a hand-waving, wild-haired teacher tried to get us to absorb "Childe Roland to the Dark Tower Came," and Louis (as in Armstrong—or Mountbatten) slipped me the copy of *Live/Dead* he'd managed to score over the holidays, told me about the Zappa concert he'd seen at the Hammersmith Odeon the week before. He zipped into Tammy Wynette songs for no reason at all—I began to think he'd committed Marlon Brando's entire performance in the new film *The Godfather* to memory—and as our teacher tried in vain to lead us into the jeweled rhapsodies of *Antony and Cleopatra*, Louis, well suited to being fifteen, intoned, "The *bhaji* [and not 'The barge'] she sat on . . ." because strange-smelling Indian restaurants were now more evident than royal vessels.

I first got to know him well when, with characteristic generosity, he invited me to come and stay with his family during "Long Leave," a break of six days in the middle of the term when boys could revisit their families (but that was too short for me to go all the way back to my parents in California). We sat in a stately expanse worthy of *Brideshead Revisited* and Louis played me the stinging, eccentric ditties of Loudon Wainwright III ("Be Careful, There's a Baby in the House") and tried to persuade me of the brilliance of Evelyn Waugh. His face turned red in the sun, and his pale skin and very fair hair seemed to rhyme with all the ancestral portraits, stretching back through centuries, in the drawing room.

When we left school for nine months before going to university, and I poured water in a Mexican restaurant to save up to ride buses from Tijuana to Titicaca, Louis went to work at a home for impoverished kids in South Africa. When I saw him again, at college, my friend was exactly the antic, pinwheeling character I'd come to cherish, grabbing me by the thighs along Oxford's High Street and always up for a summer trip to Vegas where we could try to live off the vouchers for free meals by which casinos hoped to lure the innocent. But in his time working with the children of Cape Town, I later learned, something dramatic had happened. He rarely spoke of it—and only after a long time to me, one of his oldest friends—but one day he had been lying on his bed, he said, and suddenly an overwhelming conviction had run through him, and he had risen from the bed a Christian. This wasn't an easy road to take—years of enforced chapel twice a day had made most of us think of the Gospels as the enemy, exactly what we longed to flee—and it made him sad to be set apart from the parents and siblings he so unstintingly loved, who didn't fully share his belief. But the faith he slipped into his life, like a secret business card, meant that he could be wilder and more uninhibited than ever in his explorations because, deep down, he knew precisely where he stood.

To sustain the friendship we had started in school, Louis and I began to take trips around the world, when we could save up the money—to Burma, to Turkey, to Morocco and Haiti and Cuba. Louis was the ideal traveling companion, I found, because he had a hunger for danger and drama and was strong and settled enough to be uprooted by almost nothing. His zest for adventure and unhardened delight meant that no door was closed to him; he could pick out the most attractive girl in any room—and, more amazingly, be next to that girl, one of her best friends, within minutes, as she sensed that he was fun, open-hearted, spirited and funny, but beneath that would never hassle her, because bound to a deeper, less worldly commitment.

Down the roads of the underdeveloped world we bumped, Louis usually at the wheel, planning the next party, playing me John Cipollina's strangest riffs (and sermons from the evangelical preacher he now listened to in the City), carrying himself with the élan of a schoolboy James Bond who had ended up, in his faded linen suit and Panama hat, more of a carefree, though often bedridden, Bertie Wooster. Things always happened when he was around—his impatience with feeling bored ensured they must—and every evening, as he got into his tragicomic blue djellaba to go to sleep, he'd pull out the worn black book he read every morning, too, and kneel by his bed, eyes closed.

One year, when we were in our mid-twenties, suddenly he appeared in California, and we went to the Dead's New Year's Eve concert at the Oakland Coliseum; in the early hours of the year's first morning we found ourselves winding around curving roads in the hills, next to guileless, smiling faces in bobble caps singing "Scarlet Begonias." Louis had long been fascinated by my father—an embodiment, it might seem, of everything his highly established England had seldom seen before—and perhaps he was more open then I to following the lead of some other. I came up the stairs from my bedroom one morning and found that (as on his trip ten years before) he'd sat up all night listening to my father, as my wildly colorful parent spun elaborate, riveting stories of the Albigensian heresy and Nixon's secret operations with the CIA.

Some door in me swung open as I watched my friend and saw how far true faith could be from mere piety, and how a real commitment to some religion could mean liberation as much as constraint. I could never quite buy what I heard on the evangelical tapes he played, but there was no doubt that faith had provided a frame for him to act with even more clarity and kindness than he might have done otherwise. Every time I met him, he seemed to have slipped away from his job as a managing director of Goldman Sachs to go on some barely explained Christian rescue mission—to Moldova or St. Petersburg or Tallinn (a stranger would have taken him to be a spy). He never walked past a beggar in Fez without offering him some help.

Often, inevitably, we ended up in places where Greene had been, too, but the correspondences that arose seemed only to heighten the eerie sense of possession I felt with the semi-imagined friend I'd fashioned in my head. We stepped out, one sweltering afternoon, of the little Casa Grande Hotel in Santiago de Cuba and, as soon as we got into a car, a stranger slipped in and promised to show us around; a few years later I read how Greene had stepped out of the little Casa Grande

Hotel in Santiago de Cuba, thirty-five years before we did, and, as soon as he got into a car, a stranger slipped in, promising to show him around.

I told Louis one sunlit afternoon that the essence of the Dalai Lama's teaching for non-Buddhists was contained in the line we'd read at school, from *Hamlet:* "There is nothing either good or bad, but thinking makes it so." I'd spent five years writing a study of the Dalai Lama, to address Graham Greene's questions under a different cover: how act with conscience and clarity in the midst of the world's confusions and how see things as they really are and still have faith in them? Then—we were staying in a convent on the Via Dolorosa in Jerusalem—I searched the hostel's bookshelves and found a copy of Greene's late novel, *Monsignor Quixote.* I opened the epigraph page and read, "There is nothing either good or bad, but thinking makes it so."

Louis had little time for Greene and his many doubts; faith for him was a way to allow you to act with full confidence because your foundations never wavered. So I didn't know how to explain the hauntedness I felt. All his life, I'd read, Greene had an obscure fear of seeing his house burn down. Then, when he was thirty-seven, his home really did go up in flames, during the Blitz, and he took the opportunity to leave his family behind and never really lived in a domestic setting again. One day, when I was thirty-three, I climbed upstairs in my family home and saw seventy-foot flames through every picture window. By the time the California wildfire had reduced our house and everything in it to rubble, I had decided to make my sense of belonging truly internal and go to the most clarifying society I knew, Japan, to live in a two-room flat with little on its shelves but a worn copy of *The Quiet American.*

CHAPTER 4

Yet everyone has these figures in their heads, and their presence inside and around us is often more unsettling, because more mysterious, than that of the people we meet. Henry James knows my innermost thoughts, I'd hear a friend say, to the point where I'm scared to see what he will write next; Joni Mitchell, in *Blue*, has been reading my diary, someone else would confess, and it's spooky how she knows the secrets I never tell to anyone. It might be a character in Henry James, or some actor we've never met; but everyone I know carries around such presences, which—like old loves or private faiths—hold us precisely because they are impossible to explain away.

I never wanted to seek out Greene's manuscripts or letters in research libraries; I made no conscious effort to track down those people who'd known him. He lived vividly enough inside me already, in some more shadowy place. I'd watch myself sending a long e-mail to someone I'd just met and wasn't sure I liked or trusted and hear Greene say that it was a form of "moral cowardice" to sustain a connection just because you couldn't find the right way to end it. I'd pray to some spirit I wasn't sure I believed in, on behalf of someone I cared for, and then hear Greene whisper that to enter such a relationship was to give up much more than you could hope to get in return. I'd tell myself that having a house burn down was ultimately for the best, and I'd hear him, ever-agile, note that no piety can be trusted if it answers too closely to our needs.

Sometimes, as a boy, I'd look up at my father's bookshelf and see the black-and-white framed photo there he kept of his hero, Mahatma Gandhi, striding barechested towards some righteousness he loved. Living without many possessions, universal in his loincloth, blessed with a lawyer's canny sense of theater, he might have been offering the world a model and something of a silent admonition at the same time. I shuddered a little when I learned that Gandhi was born on the same day of the year as Greene, thirty-five years before, with the result (which might have caused Greene to smile) that October 2 is now known to some as the "International Day of Non-Violence."

∴

I had already been deep in Greene for more than fifteen years when, finally, one midsummer day of coastal fog, our house in California seeming to sit above the world, removed by the clouds below it, I picked up his very first published novel, spookily entitled *The Man Within*. I'd never been much interested in the early books, which Greene himself had furiously renounced, and it was the man of the middle years, holding himself to rigorous account, who transfixed me; but now, picking up the small blue volume, I felt as rattled as if a stranger were shouting obscenities in my face.

A boy is running across a down as darkness falls—this was how the novel, completed when Greene was just twenty-four, begins. He is being pursued by a gang of smugglers—his father's gang—whom he has betrayed to the authorities; his pursuers, therefore, are being pursued, too, by the law. As he stumbles through the gloom, he sees a light ahead and comes upon a kind of fairy-tale cottage in the dark. In front of it stands a "slim upstrained candle-flame, a woman," pointing a gun at him.

In time she agrees to take him in, and when he asks her why there's a coffin in her room, she explains that the man inside it had been a quasi-father to her, as well as a tormentor. The girl, Elizabeth, is nineteen, younger even than the boy, but soon, very soon, given shelter by her, the boy comes to feel she's holy, his redemption. "She is a saint, he thought," I read on page 50, and then, twelve pages later, "'She is a saint,' he thought." She gives him a sense of peace—of safety—he's known only when listening to music, or, oddly, at school.

But in order to earn his place in her sanctuary, he has to go back out into the world; Elizabeth urges him to testify publicly against his former gangmates in the local court. So he heads out into the dark once more and makes his way to the nearest town, and an inn named after a goat. He tells the people he meets there that his name is Absalom, like that of the character in the Bible who tries to kill his father, David. He picks up a young and easy woman on the arm of an older man, but—as she notes bitterly—spoils even their brief coupling with his overanxious conscience. There is no justice in the world, he comes to see as the smugglers are acquitted, while pure Elizabeth is characterized in court as a harlot; yet some iron law of punishment within ensures that he must pay in some way for his betrayal of the criminals.

The constant sense that haunts the novel of a boy torn between the romantic in him and the would-be cynic—the believer and the devil—is perhaps not so unusual; but the violence of the feeling is intense. "There's another man within me," run the very first words of Greene's first published novel, in an epigraph from the seventeenth-century essayist Sir Thomas Browne, "and he's angry with me." Again and again we read, of this first protagonist, "He was, he knew, embarrassingly made up of two persons, the sentimental, bullying, desiring child and another more stern critic." The first novel Greene ever wrote, never published, was, bizarrely, the story of a black boy born unhappily to white parents in England. The same Greene who could write with such urbanity about the "other" Graham Greene who impersonated him around the world could apprehend the other within himself— his lifelong theme and antagonist—only with a sense of near-despair.

∴

I knew Greene," my friend Paul began telling me, one warm afternoon in December, as we sipped tea after lunch on his expansive estate in Hawaii, and he pointed out the twenty kinds of bamboo on the property (a modern-day version, I thought, of the house that Greene's cousin Robert Louis Stevenson had made on Samoa). Half a dozen geese clucked along the path, and in the bungalow where Paul did his writing, fierce tribal masks from Angola and the Pacific Islands grinned down unnervingly; on one desk sat a signed Helmut Newton print, of a woman in a black hat and veil fellating a fully clothed man, his face out of view.

"But you couldn't really know him," he went on. "He didn't want you to. He never inhabited places. He lived in flats; he didn't like to be at home."

They had first come into contact when Greene, in a characteristic act of largesse, had offered some words of public praise for Paul's first book of travels, *The Great Railway Bazaar*, perhaps because he saw strong echoes in it of his own early book and first commercial success, *Stamboul Train*. A train is a perfect setting for a story, Greene had realized, since every one of the passengers is carrying his own secrets, unguessed at by the others, and the setting is always changing. The backdrop shifts, propulsively, even as the figures in the foreground sink deeper and deeper into their half-curtained dramas. Greene was always eager to help younger writers, especially if they seemed to lack official connections.

"The first time we met," Paul now recalled, "we talked about infidelity. I bared my soul to him. I'd had this image, before we met, of a power figure, shamanic. But he didn't type, he didn't drive, he couldn't boil an egg.

"He wasn't much older than my father. But he seemed to come from a different age. I wanted his blessing. The older writer is always a father figure. And I needed approval from him, guidance from him. I wanted to be him." A few years later, Paul had actually written a novel, *Picture Palace*, in which his protagonist, an elderly American photographer, Maude Coffin Pratt, begins her story by flying across the Atlantic to meet Graham Greene in his favorite lair, the downstairs bar at the Ritz.

"The novelist's eyes were pale and depthless," Paul had

written, through Maude, "with a curious icy light that made me think of a creature who can see in the dark, the more so because they were also the intimidating eyes of a blind man, with a hypnotist's unblinking stare." Greene comes across to his visitor as many things at once: a father confessor, a louche clergyman, a wise old lion guarding his secrets. But most of all—and this was what so many found in Greene—he seems to her somehow a reflection of herself. Soon after they meet, she sees him as "an older brother, a fellow sufferer." But as the evening goes on, she comes to feel that, for all their differences in gender, age and nationality, really she is looking at herself. She wants to take his picture, to make it the final piece in her coming retrospective, because, she realizes, strangely, "it's the next best thing to taking my own picture."

∴

The whole point of an adopted parent, I'd often thought, is that you can have him to yourself. He's a figment of your imagination, in a sense, someone you've created to satisfy certain needs, so he's always there, in your head, at your disposal. Real parents have lives to attend to, lives beyond our understanding, and they commit, most of all, the sin of being real; they're human and distractible and fallible. Sometimes we seem to create ourselves in the light of their mistakes.

But the parents we construct in our minds—the ones we enlist for our purposes—are more like the people we want to be, or at least the ones whose affinities we gladly acknowledge. Someone says you look like your father, and you wince, or recoil; the great project of self-creation has clearly failed.

Someone says that you sound like that eminent novelist, and you're flattered. You've followed intuition, or yourself.

With Greene, of course, this could never be so straightforward; I'd already come across at least six books in which a contemporary writer had come to feel so under his spell that he (or occasionally she) had woven stories around the man within his head, and usually they were stories about young writers growing possessed by him to the point where he seemed to take over their lives (most eerily in Alan Judd's novel *The Devil's Own*, whose protagonist becomes Greene, in effect, and hears a phantom scribbling whenever he picks up a pen). Greene got into people's heads and souls—under their skin—as contemporaries of his who were often more highly regarded (Aldous Huxley, Evelyn Waugh, George Orwell) rarely did with quite the same intensity. When Paul told him that his wife had taken up with another man while he was traveling, Greene asked if Paul had left her. "No," Paul said. "I would have done," Greene replied. And then, a little later, "And I'd have regretted it."

That doubleness was itself part of what Greene handed down to so many of us (Paul had later written a series of books, riveting and unsettling, about the secret life he might or might not have led). I remembered how the Vietnamese spy I'd met in Saigon had said, when asked how he could send parallel reports to *Time* and to Ho Chi Minh, "The truth? What truth? Two truths—both are true."

Yet the existence of all these others who felt such a kinship with Greene made me feel doubly uneasy; the sacred trust of friendship is that you see something in the other that no one else can see, and he the same with you. And the nature of affinity (and in Greene's world, of love) is that it stands to no reason at all. "That's another mystery," a police chief declares in *The*

Power and the Glory, "how you think you've seen people—
and places—before. Was it in a dream or in a past life?"

∴

I did dream of Greene, more than once, most often when I
was up in the air, between places; the very lack of drama
in our meetings confirmed my sense of him as an unsought
familiar.

I met him one evening in a town just south of Santa
Barbara—this is what I saw once, in a plane above the
Pacific—and we had dinner together and drove towards the
town where my parents lived in life. It wasn't hard to talk to
him, yet everything I did ended up wrong somehow. At dinner,
lost in conversation, I'd let him pay (as he took pains to remind
me). "Can I get you a drink?" I'd asked, to make amends.

"A drink, then, yes."

He was driving a large white SUV, very precisely (though in
life, a part of me knew, he couldn't drive at all). We stopped
near a place on the beach. He ordered drinks for himself, and
we met in an ill-lit bar. As it came on for 11:00 p.m., Hiroko
appeared, my mother, but I had to tell them to stand by while
I took care of my distinguished guest.

I asked him about Scott Fitzgerald; the scene reminded me
of a moment in *The Last Tycoon*. He confessed to liking no
American writer.

"They're completely different," I agreed, and he shook his
head slowly. He got more drinks and started lamenting a biography that had just come out about one Ben Jackson. A hero
of Empire, in his forties, and yet—Greene said—a modern
writer had got him all wrong.

He drank and drank; I recalled that even in his eighties he could drain two bottles without effect. But now he looked wasted, quite vulnerable, and at times he disappeared. I realized I'd have to drive the few blocks back to his hotel. I got into the new SUV and I couldn't move; the brake was on.

Then I started moving around a roundabout, and I thought I glimpsed him, but he was gone. He'd be angry, I thought, if he knew I was looking for him—even though I'd paid for the drinks—and I began to feel I'd failed in every part of the evening. I'd tried not to ask him anything that would put him out, but now he was drunk, unsteady, and I'd lost him in a place I knew he'd never like.

∴

In 2004—the hundredth anniversary of Greene's birth—the man was suddenly everywhere again, as if he hadn't died thirteen years before. The third and final volume of a huge authorized biography by Norman Sherry came out, and others who'd known or heard of him emerged to offer their own anti-gospels, or settling of accounts; a group of young Americans was settling into a Green Zone in Iraq, talking of local forces with whom they could make alliances and determined to remake Mesopotamia with the latest ideas of Boston. A new film of *The Quiet American* had recently been completed, but it had been screened for its producers on September 10, 2001, and then had to be held back for more than a year because it described the future (the present) much too well.

In honor of the centenary, his publishers decided to bring out all Greene's novels in new editions, and I was asked to write an introduction for a collection of his short fiction. I'd never much liked his stories—they were too angry and private, often, and he didn't have the space to develop the unexpected sympathies and painful paradoxes of the novels—but to read the shorter work all through gave me a chance to see him in the round: from the raging young man imprisoned within England and gray corridors, who loves to write of murder; to the much more anguished and self-incriminating explorer of the middle years (who writes of suicide); to, at last, the mellow ironist in his sixties who has learned to smile a little at what he cannot change and, approaching death, to cherish youth with new delight precisely for its unknowingness.

As I sat in the house my mother had rebuilt after the fire, however—my father had passed away by then—suddenly something curious happened, which took me back to a hotel room in Bolivia, and Easter Island. Uncalled for, and without wanting to, I began writing Greene stories instead of reading them. Out they came, from nowhere I could recognize, in a single burst, day after day: now I was imagining an old classmate of his, visited by a young biographer, and telling stories of the schoolboy Greene that the biographer (and we) cannot begin to assess as truth or fiction. Now I was imagining a London cabbie talking about his predicament in life: his parents, a well-meaning Mr. and Mrs. Greene, have baptized him "Graham" and whenever he tells someone his name, she thinks he's having her on or attempting a not very good joke. Yet he cannot change his name without altering his destiny.

Now I was seeing him set up a counseling center in Oxford with a likable rogue he's met from (where else?) Bolivia; now he was following a young love to El Salvador, and losing her to two new passions she develops—for the Church and social justice—with which he knows he can never compete.

I couldn't begin to tell where any of these stories came from; I sat at my desk every morning and transcribed them, as if taking dictation. When they were in front of me, I didn't know what to make of them (he'd never been to Java, I knew, and he couldn't have met Ho Chi Minh in Paris in 1923). But somehow, I came to think, he became the way I could unlock something in the imagination; he was the way I could get into places in myself that were otherwise well-defended.

Perhaps, I reflected, that was one of the less obvious things we shared. "Whenever I talk about myself," he'd told his long-time companion Yvonne, "I wear a mask." To which, in a very different context, referring to acting, his friend (and companion in Haiti), Peter Brook, had noted, "The fact that the mask gives you something to hide behind makes it unnecessary for you to hide."

Like Greene, I suspect, I'd never had much time for memoir; it was too easy to make yourself the center—even the hero—of your story and to use recollection as a way to forgive yourself for everything. Besides, there was a falsity in trying (or pretending) to soothe the rush of often contradictory and inexplicable events in every life into a kind of pattern with easily decipherable meanings and even a happy, redemptive ending. But the phantom stories startled—and intrigued—me because they reminded me how, in every book, there is another text, written in invisible ink between the lines, that may be telling the real story, of what the words evade.

CHAPTER 5

I was eight years old when my mother and father moved us to California. I looked around me on the dusty, unpaved lane where we ended up—"Banana Road," as it was unofficially called—and felt bewildered. There were dry brush mountains at the end of the path, and a boy called Duane was showing me how to look out for rattlesnakes and turn over a spider to see the red hourglass on the stomach that revealed a poisonous black widow. There were almost no houses within view, and only nine months before our arrival, a huge wildfire—the Coyote Fire—had swept through the area, taking down one hundred houses and leaving the slopes as charred and ugly as a man who's just had his hair hacked off.

I could hardly believe that, only a few months earlier, I'd been running along Winchester Road in Oxford, past long rows of semidetached porridge-grey houses, from which Russian or Polish or Arabic drifted out, or the elaborate études our local member of Parliament played on the piano deep into the night, in his second-floor bachelor flat. Almost everyone had known everyone else there—most were attached to

St. Antony's College, named after one of the first Western ascetics to wander off into the wilderness—and there was a sense that things were done as they had been done for seven hundred years or more. Eager visitors came to see the sights and I tagged along as my parents showed them the radical new statue of the risen Lazarus in New College, or the sculpture of Percy Bysshe Shelley, naked and washed up on the shore, tucked into a late Victorian dome in the college called University.

And now we were in this vast open space—736 Coyote Road—where the future was much more visible than the past, and I was waiting with a yellow Yogi Bear lunch box in my hand for a school bus to take me on an hour-long circuit every morning, around the sycamore canyons and eucalyptus-lined hills, to a school in the pastoral expanse of Hope Ranch. In Oxford my friends and I had all enrolled at the Dragon School, where, like generations of boys before us, we began Latin in the first grade, Greek in the second; here I was in a world I hardly recognized, except from sitcoms on TV, where the boys had crew cuts and braces on their teeth and girls rode their horses in the lazy afternoons through leafy streets called Via Tranquila or Via Esperanza. On Sadie Hawkins Day we were all driven to the beach, where "California Girls" was playing on a radio, and as the teachers got to know me, they didn't know which grade to place me in, I seemed so small in some ways and so well drilled in others. In Oxford we'd been told that the word for love was *amo*.

I'd always taken for granted that I was English; I sounded and lived just like the Campbells and Kirkwoods down the road. At SS Philip and James' Church of England Aided Primary School, I'd taken on the part of Joseph in the Christmas pageant and every summer I'd eagerly headed off to the medieval fair in St. Giles', in the shadow of the memorial to the three sixteenth-century Protestants who had been burned in the street for heresy against "the Church of Rome." It was a very bounded, safe world, Oxford in 1963, where someone might say that she'd just run into Mrs. Greene, the novelist's wife, who lived across from the Ashmolean, and the family friend who'd take over the Dickensian job of being my "guardian" had been to the same college as the novelist.

Sometimes, I'd walk proudly along the street with my father to his office on Canterbury Road, three minutes from our home. He'd let me sort out all the magazines that had assembled over the past few months—the *New Statesman, Encounter, The Listener*—and I'd organize them according to date and title and make great piles along the floor. It seemed like one of those puzzles that appeared at the back of my comic books; it was only much later—perhaps too late—that I saw how much the names on the covers of those magazines (George Orwell, Aldous Huxley, E. M. Forster, Graham Greene) might mean to a young man from the suburbs of Bombay who'd always dreamed of living among the ancient cloisters and tolling bells he'd read about with such constancy from afar.

∴

In the pictures, when I look at them now, I see a full-lipped man, with bright, compelling eyes, dandling on his lap a baby with huge head and careless smile. His delight in his son is obvious as he looks back at the lens with a natural, unintimidated sense of command. My father told me rich, many-chambered stories before I went to bed each night—Sita and Ravana from

The Ramayana mixed with all that he'd got from Tennyson and Shakespeare—and he taught me to read the newspaper almost as soon as I began to talk. By the time I was five, I was filling my green exercise books with long stories about witches, wizards and dragons, though making sure (I was my father's son) that the goodies always voted Labour, and the baddies were given away by their support of the Conservatives.

As I grew older, though, and began to read the essays he'd written as a very young man—startlingly confident and fluent pieces on utilitarianism and the end of the British Empire, on Rousseau and Condorcet—I realized that I had no sense at all of where my father came from. He was a mystery I could never solve. He'd grown up in the unglamorous outskirts of Bombay, son of a worker at the Ford Motor Company and a girl who had borne him when she was fifteen. None of his six siblings seemed to share his interests or temperament, and when first I saw the single room they'd slept in—I was visiting my parents' homeland at seventeen—I could not imagine how anyone could study in so cramped a space.

My grandmother sat on a long sofa in the small flat, doors thrown open so that everyone could come in and enjoy her gregarious protection, and chattered away in a fluent Tamil that my father, her firstborn, could barely speak (English was the realm he inhabited). She'd never had enough time for taking classes—bearing children through her teens—and my own mother had grown up in a separate universe, amidst the cosmopolitan comforts of South Bombay, with parents who knew all about Cambridge, Massachusetts, and London from having studied there.

But my father had become a teacher at the celebrated University of Bombay by the time he was eighteen (my mother, a year younger, one of his first students), and by then he was already famous around town for the essays he wrote on *The Tempest* and his ability to stand before any audience and talk without notes, hypnotic, on almost any topic from Tolstoy to Plotinus. He won India's only Rhodes Scholarship in 1950, and at Oxford he became president of the Oxford Union, arguing for Shaw's claim that "progress depends on the unreasonable man," while surrounded by busts of the many other Union presidents who had gone on to become presidents in some larger sphere. In his final exams he did so well, he won a research fellowship to deepen his studies into Gandhi and the philosophical roots of nonviolence.

Later, when I was growing up, he would tell me how he'd been taken, as a boy himself, to see Ramana Maharshi, the famous mystic—also an Iyer, as it happened, part of our priestly clan—who'd lived in a cave for seventeen years, practicing "self-enquiry" and communicating mostly through silence (I'd meet him later in the guru based on him in Somerset Maugham's *The Razor's Edge*, and the essay, fascinated though open-ended, Maugham wrote about their encounter, "The Saint"). But such unworldly influences my father had balanced and made more rigorous by reading Hobbes and Hume and Locke, as well as the English poets. It was as if his life was to be consecrated to the joining of the spiritual and the political domains; and by linking them together, he could perhaps join East and West as well, separated, for the time being, as he'd written in his first book, by a "glass curtain."

I suppose a main character in a Graham Greene novel might have pretended to mock my father for having more belief than a traditional Englishman admits to; he was an idealist and a vegetarian, like the reformist Smiths whom Greene's alter ego

Brown keeps laughing at in *The Comedians*. He'd been taught, as my mother and so many in their generation and before had been, that the natural culmination of any good Indian student in British India was Britain, but when he got there, he'd found that the place he'd been taught to admire was trapped in a long tradition of skepticism and "on the other hand"s, the stuff out of which Greene had formed his negative creed. The ambition that had brought him there was exactly what wasn't always welcome, and someone who could rattle off passages from Milton and the King James Bible—and then link them to a text in Tibetan Buddhism—could seem too emphatic and eager to make a point (or an impression).

So here we were now on the farthest edge of the New World, where my father had been invited to join a think tank, the Center for the Study of Democratic Institutions, at which philosophers from around the globe would gather to discuss, quite literally, how to make a new kind of city on a hill, and put together a fresh version of the *Encyclopædia Britannica*. We were driven, on a visit, between a stately pair of gates and through what seemed a tropical Eden to a Mediterranean villa, commanding fifty-six acres of eucalyptus trees above the ocean, the sky so blue it hurt my eyes, and told that we had arrived in "the Athens of the West." It wasn't impossible to believe.

One year after we arrived in Santa Barbara, we bought a new house on a hill, alone on a ridge halfway up what were called "the mountains" and looking out over the white-walled, red-tiled town below to Santa Cruz Island in the distance. It had been a hippie house—kids had dropped acid here and then driven their VWs off the slope, into the cushioning beds of ice plant—and even when we bought it, it sat outside the city limits, far from anyone's jurisdiction. Our water came up to us from a well, reached by a jolting, forty-five-minute drive into the valley tucked below, along another unpaved road, and in the evenings the wind often howled around us at eighty miles an hour, rattling our windows and almost blowing us over as we struggled in from the car.

One night the winds ripped the whole terrace off the side of the house overlooking the city and propelled it across the roof till it lay, grotesquely twisted, on the mountainside. My mother, waking up, and about to step out to feed the cat, almost walked into thin air.

The house had been built by a fundamentalist who had taken very seriously the biblical injunction to build his house "upon a rock"; he had found a large boulder up amidst the brush, and without benefit of foundations—or architectural experience—laid down a two-story structure. Its rising roof gave it the look of a ship that was about to sail off across the billowing clouds that so often separated us from the town; it seemed as if we had left all moorings behind, to enter some realm of unfettered speculation.

∴

I felt, at some level that I could not articulate then, as if we had stepped out of a cozy drawing-room comedy, written by Greene in a holiday mood, and into some Old Testament text about the end—or the beginning—of the world. But for my father, I later realized, he could not have arrived in a better place at a better time. His deepest commitment had always been to possibility, the mystic's belief that there's a better life hidden within the one we see; the maxim he most loved to cite to students was from Greene's favorite, Unamuno, about how, to achieve the impossible, one must attempt the absurd. He had even named his only child after the Buddha and the fifteenth-century Italian Neo-Platonist who had written an "Oration on the Dignity of Man."

And now he was in a state that seemed given over to unlimited potential, discussing *The Symposium* with some of the world's most interesting thinkers in the mornings and at night walking in candlclit rallies for peace with Joan Baez and other young champions of hope. He was invited to teach at the local university, along with my philosopher mother, and soon they were both finding that students in California in the '60s, unlike the students they'd taught at Oxford, weren't embarrassed about professing an interest in their studies, didn't believe they had all the answers, were sometimes almost touchingly open to transformation. Three hundred, four hundred kids started crowding into the lecture halls where my father was talking on Bakunin and Thomas Paine (and, perhaps, the *Perry Mason* show he'd watched on TV the previous night), binding them all together into a soaring synthesis; he began holding his office hours in an all-night coffee shop, so that students could bring him their questions, their hopes or their plans for as long as they wished. Sometimes, he would still be talking, on Coleridge and Pythagoras, as the sun began to show above the far-off ridge at 6:00 a.m.

It was those from the Old World who had the keenest sense, I thought, of how much could be done in this hopeful and accommodating society and how, in fact, the very principles of classical philosophy could be given new wings and life in this place so unconcerned with history. Christopher Isherwood, Greene's distant cousin, came to our local Hindu temple to talk about how he'd decided to devote his literary energies to

the Indian swami he'd met here; he'd seen through the deca-
dence of Europe, the worn-out skepticisms of England, and
this life seemed more exciting to him. Felix Greene, the first
cousin with whom Graham had grown up in England, helped
to found a mystical community in the desert east of Los Angeles where Aldous Huxley, Greene's contemporary and long-
time fascination, could deepen his research into the perennial
philosophy. Somerset Maugham, Greene's most obvious prec-
edent, had told Isherwood, down the road, that his great wish
as he approached seventy was to go to India to study Shankara.

When my parents took me down to the campus in the
warm, subtropical evenings, I could hear wild guitar riffs and
Oedipal screams—the Doors—floating out of the basketball
gym and across to where the Pacific lapped against the shore
just in front of the university lagoon; a little later, the students
would burn down our local Bank of America and more or less
announce that they were fashioning a new world from scratch,
whether in preparation for the future or just celebration of the
powers of eternal youth, nobody much troubled to say.

But for a little boy it was all a bit unsettling, and perhaps
more so in the presence of a father with vivid and esoteric
views, and no siblings to cushion the effect. I didn't know what
to make of the two pictures of Western occultists my father
kept on his bookshelves, next to Gandhi, and I couldn't follow
his frequent references to demons and magicians, a mysterious psychic sphere that filled the invisible spaces around us.
And the California I knew seemed so far from time and even
reality that it felt more a vision of a place—a cluster of visions,
only sometimes overlapping—than anywhere one could learn
one's ABCs.

Yet strong fathers are also often the ones with the strongest
readiness to give their children a solid education, if only so

as to fortify the family against the world (or maybe it's just a way of having a second chance?). And as I sat in our lonely house on the ridge, playing with my favorite toys (numbers), I noticed that the dollar was so strong against the pound— America had clearly taken over as the dominant power—that I could fly back to Oxford, resume my studies at the Dragon (which, conveniently, took in boarders as well as day students) and fly back to see my parents three times a year for less than it cost to carry my lunchbox with the crustless cucumber sandwiches to Hope Ranch every morning.

I didn't stop to think about how hard it might be for parents to give up their only child to rival authorities across the world; I didn't bother to reflect that the smaller party can abandon the larger, as much as the other way round. I raised the idea with my parents and they assented, because they had seen how much I might forget if I stayed in this fresh and unformed society. They had been at least as concerned as I when I described, aged nine, what my twelve-year-old California classmates were planning to do next summer on the beach with Diane.

A curious decision, perhaps, for a boy of nine, but empty spaces can be difficult for a little boy alone and maybe I sensed that my parents, raised on Britain in India, were at times as perplexed as I by this unanchored new world we'd entered, and undefended against the different forms innocence and worldliness took over here. A world that knew itself seemed safer than one in a perpetual state of becoming—at least until I hit fifteen—and even algebra teachers flinging hard blackboard erasers at us and pulling us by the hair could seem more knowable than the vast open spaces of this world without boundaries.

So we got into our small blue Plymouth Valiant and drove

down the intercontinental freeway to Los Angeles International Airport. A woman in a stylish uniform took me over from there and put my passport and other papers into a plastic bag. Then I was waving and waving at my mother and father, and turning around to follow the woman into the front of a plane. My parents were left to drive the hundred miles home by themselves, while I headed back to the strange, cloistered world of Victorian England.

∴

At the other end, a wispy-haired man in a tweed jacket with patches on the elbows was waiting to lead me into an estate car (the previous day I'd have called it a "station wagon"), along with other boys coming from Buenos Aires, Nairobi, all the imperial postings, and to deposit us in our new red-brick houses around Bardwell Road. The room where I would soon sleep was called Pterodactyl, named, like all the rooms in School House, after a creature long extinct, and in those early days all I could think of was California. I buried myself under my blankets after "Lights Out" and under threat of getting thwacked on the backside with a tennis shoe, fiddled with my tiny transistor radio to try to catch a college football game on the Armed Forces Radio Service, broadcasting from Germany. My only piece of home was an NFL handbook that soon I had read so often I could recite Raymond Berry's touchdown statistics as fluently as if it were Kipling's "If—"

Yet children are often much readier to adapt than their parents are, and before long I was putting on my blue corduroy shorts, my grey Aertex shirt and my blue corduroy jacket—all with "S. P. R. Iyer" in green Cash's name tapes sewed into them by my mother—and was happily flinging conjugations of the Greek irregular verb βαιυω (εβην, βηθι, βω; βαιην, βηναι, βας) at my classmates instead of curses. The Dragon was the rare school that allowed boys to bring teddy bears with them to their beds. But, wise to the dangers of life in the trenches, I took along only a stunt bear, so that the creature I really cared for could remain safe at home, out of view.

∴

School House was, of course, the name of the building where Graham Greene lived, too, both as a student at Berkhamsted and, in holidays, as son of the headmaster; the name itself might have stood for the universe of his fiction, where even in their forties, Old Boys are putting on the ties of schools not quite their own, reminiscing about faraway teachers, even urging other alumni, met at the club in West Africa, to send reports or love poems back to the old school magazine. In Greene's day, the names of students newly fallen in war were recited every day in chapel (the two hundredth to be killed, by a horrible irony, was called "Dear," the five hundredth "Good"). In our day, the war was long behind us—Empire had been seriously wounded in the First War and then killed off in the Second—but tall memorials stood above our playing fields, with the names of the dead all around them, and everywhere we turned were plaques and poppies.

On Sunday afternoons hundreds of seats were laid out in School Hall, so we could watch *Zulu* and *The Bridge on the River Kwai* and learn about what loyalty to king and country meant, and how to suffer silently; on Saturday afternoons, a teacher read to us from *Esprit de Corps* and *Stiff Upper Lip*, Lawrence Durrell's stories of life in the Foreign Office, to prepare us for our own detachment abroad. We had to run through a long line of freezing cold showers every morning at dawn, though, by some topsy-turvy logic, the number of warm baths we could take was limited to two a week and had to be overseen by young female Matrons.

In chapel we sang, "There is a green hill far away," and I thought, inevitably, of our house, now painted yellow, on the ridge in California, on the far side of the world; on the last day of every term, just as my mother and her friends had done at Cathedral and John Connon School in Bombay, we all but shouted out William Blake's lines about building a new Jerusalem in "England's green and pleasant land." When I was allowed "out of bounds," occasionally, to buy sweets from the shop round the corner from where I'd grown up, it was to think of the dentist down the road, in the same street where Graham Greene's wife and children lived. The name of our school magazine was *The Draconian*.

∴

Once a year, perhaps, through an elaborate lottery system, each of us had a chance to win the ultimate prize: freedom from school lunch. If a letter was chosen close enough to the "I" in "Iyer"—I can remember even now the sensation of crowding around the magic box in the room lined with lockers—I was given a small paper bag and told, at 10:40 on a Sunday morning, that I didn't have to show up again till dinner at

6:15. Inside the bag was a small packet of potato chips, a Penguin chocolate bar, an apple and a 6½-ounce bottle of Coke. Fully aware of how special a luxury this was, I ran upstairs to my room, searched around for the compass in my pencil box, jabbed a few holes in the rusty bottle top and proceeded to sip the elixir through the pinpricks for the next four hundred and fifty-four minutes.

Outsiders would seldom understand why we would later, with complete sincerity, call our years at school the best days of our lives. But we were situated within a very clearly ordered universe, in which an omnipotent authority determined everything. Every tiny pleasure felt earned, legitimate, and we always knew exactly where we stood. We were learning how to live with other boys, how to work with them and give them space, how to gauge their secrets as spies (and novelists and priests) do; our regimental comrades, as they quickly came to seem, would remain our closest friends through life, even if we couldn't always tell how much we knew them (or they us).

The second biggest dorm in the school was called "Gunga Din," in honor of the native water bearer in Kipling who dies to save a British officer's life; on Sunday mornings, we assembled again in our classrooms and wrote twice-folded blue Air Letters to our parents. "Dear Mummy and Daddy," we wrote, "this week Cherwell beat Linton 3–1. You can imagine how excited we all were! Reader-Harris's parents are taking him out for tea next month—and he's invited me to come! In Divinity we're doing the Pharisees and the Gallic Wars are really galling! The School Play this term is *Oliver!*, about the boy who asked for more. But Podge asked for less last week, and he got six of the best with a tennis shoe."

In English class, they taught us about a whisky priest, who

drank and fathered a baby and forgot his prayers; when he offered Mass, the only bread he had to offer was from his mistress's oven. His parishioners were the other unwashed sinners in his prison cell. Perhaps we understood this somewhat, by intuition, as we headed back to our own cells: simple broken humanity was the sacrament, and even a holy man was "just one criminal among a herd of criminals." The rest of the world—the places of need and desperation that we were being trained to go out and administer—lived in a realm as barren and magical as that of the Gospels.

And then, overnight, as it seemed, the eighty-four days were up and I was walking down the steps of TWA 761 into the born-again sunshine of California once more, and the relieved indulgence of my parents. My father was explaining the symbolism of *Sgt. Pepper,* his eyes bright with mischief, to his students, and serious young philosophers, prom queens from the beach towns to the south—now called "Radha" and "Parvati"—were asking him earnest questions about *Walden* and "Kubla Khan."

Mountain lions could sometimes be seen in the dry hills through the window in my father's study; a mother bear had been spotted with her cub up the road. We might have been in one of the cowboy-and-Indian movies we'd so excitedly devoured on TV in Oxford (though now the Indians were of a somewhat different kind and the cowboys were mostly shy men from the south, speaking Spanish). Sometimes fires broke out on the ridges up the road—humans were surely never meant to live in wilds like these—and those who had taken my father's course on anarchist thought might note that you had to get rid of the old if a new order were ever to come into being.

∴

"No," I said, one day, many years later, in another small room in an old island empire, when Hiroko asked; it wasn't really the fact that I'd instinctively given the name "Mr. Brown" to the little sketch I'd written, imagining seeing Greene in Havana (or the fact that "Brown" was the name of his protagonist in *Brighton Rock* and *The Comedians,* his recurrent nom de guerre); it wasn't the fact that he traveled—all of us had been taught to take off across the world, and for me as for him, travel was mostly a way to see more clearly the questions and shadows it was easy to look past at home. It was that he was always on the move in some deeper sense, never ready to assume he had the last word, reflexively able to see around the corner of his beliefs and to recall how he and his world looked to the person on the far side of the street.

Always there was a dance in him between evasion and an almost ruthless candor, his instinct for privacy and his need to purge himself of his secrets on the page; he was one of those men who would often tell more to his unmet readers than to his oldest friends. He almost had to guard his public life, in fact, in order to have more to offer, less compromised, in his private; the less you let out freely to every stranger—California had taught me this, along with many of the other laws of restraint—the more and deeper the material you had to share when it most mattered.

But there was something subtler going on beyond all this: he knew what it was to animate a dialogue, quivering and uncertain, connecting the two worlds he moved between, each not knowing how much to distrust or be fascinated by the other. He knew how to keep alive the demands and intensity of faith, by not really being part of any congregation, yet refusing to stake out the easy ground of a nonbeliever. He saw that he was in part the schoolmaster whose face he surely recognized whenever he caught his blurred features in a train window— and a boy committed to forging his own way in opposition to that schoolmaster, his father. Life would and could be spent in movement, in process, not settling to any fixity or doctrine, but sensing that the human challenge was something much more profound and unassimilable. So much so, in fact, that even saints might despair of figuring out the riddle and the ache.

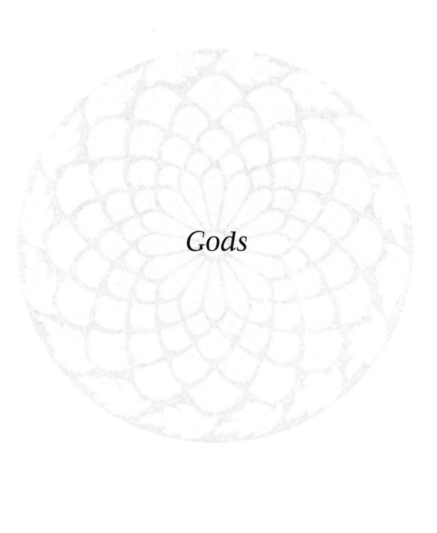

Gods

CHAPTER 6

W e were driving—well, to make a critical distinction, "being driven"—down unpaved roads across the highlands of Ethiopia, and we were being told that the eleven rock-cut churches of Lalibela were not far away, just an hour or a day or two. We had come here, Louis and I, to experience Christmas in the ancient country and we wanted to get to Lalibela on New Year's Eve, six days before the Orthodox Christmas was observed, on Epiphany. Along the road there were rusted tanks and all the debris of a recently concluded civil war; when we arrived at a village just before night fell, we were told that bandits were all around and sure to attack if we continued. Behind us in the aging white Toyota were two cans of kerosene, guaranteed to asphyxiate us if somehow we survived the road itself.

After another long day of driving, we slipped into tiny rooms in the pitch dark and fell into a deep sleep. When I walked out next morning at dawn, it was to see dozens, hundreds of believing souls, all in white, gathered on a hilltop, while below them thickly bearded priests, in purple raiment, carrying leathery

Bibles the size of a human hand, moaned and chanted from their holy books. The bright winter sun rose from behind the faraway mountains; light began to stream through the cross-shaped openings in the churches; grave, piercing faces from the Book of Kings held our own, impossible to ignore. Hundreds of pilgrims looked back at them, burning-eyed, no sign of fatigue or weakness after walking three weeks or more to be in the holy site.

"This is Golgotha," a deacon said, walking us round the site as the morning freshened. "This is Nazareth. We call this the River Jordan." The New Jerusalem had been built here, in the stronghold of Ethiopia's high mountains, to give sustenance to those who could not hope to get to the Old Jerusalem after it had been taken over by invaders.

We walked and walked and I, who had suffered through years of having to read the Gospel of Matthew in Greek and writing essays about the trial of Jesus, felt, almost for the first time, what lay behind all the symbols and the pitiful reductions; faith itself could be a solace, an exaltation, regardless of the everyday terms and icons with which we tried to encourage (or ensnare) it. This country was as bare as any I had seen, beyond the point of poverty, trying to surface again after seventeen years of dictatorship, and all it seemed to have was the hope in the priests' intense chanting, the light in the eyes of the people who had come here, as to Heaven. To stand on the hillside in the dawn and join in the thronged prayers was to step out of the moment, for a second, and disappear inside what the poets we had read at school had taught us to call "Eternity."

∴

My upbringing had left me at a little distance from both the wisdom of the East, as I heard it in my parents' home, and from the secret black book that Louis pulled out every morning and evening; like most little boys, I loved to define myself by everything I thought I could see through. Yet it was impossible not to be moved by everything the cross had brought into being here, in the eyes of people who held to their traditions as to hope itself, and the feeling that they passed on like a holy contagion.

If anything, in fact, the power of worship and the sense of purpose it created were more visible in this emptiness. There were no lights in the little settlement where we'd slept and, in the dining room, on New Year's Eve, only three other travelers, from Switzerland, had joined us for a meager dinner. But now, as we began to drive away from the chants and Bibles, back into the world, we were surrounded by hundreds of worshippers, rail thin and fragile, walking, walking, in straight lines, while dressed in flimsy, almost transparent robes, towards the churches for Epiphany.

Our driver had never been on the road before; he seemed, in truth, barely to have been behind the wheel of a car before. Three weeks earlier he had been in the army. Now he sat, with great erectness and pride—he might have been an Ethiopian Mandela, with his cropped grey hair and ancient face—and gunned the Land Cruiser at hostile speeds around blind turns.

"Slower! What are you doing—trying to kill us?" Louis shouted, a little like the London merchant I remembered from Greene's *Stamboul Train*.

The driver caught my eyes in his rearview mirror. "Sir, your friend is very strict. More strict than military."

"He is," I acknowledged. "He just came from Kenya. Some of his friends were killed there. In an accident. He's jumpy."

I hoped the mention of his country's neighbor might be enough; with its sixteen hundred years of unbroken tradition, and almost complete freedom from European control, Ethiopia was always keen to assert its distance from the rest of Africa. But I couldn't tell what, if anything, it meant to our driver; he stared with new intensity at the road and pushed his foot down, roaring around an army truck and swerving desperately back as we rounded a turn and found another truck barreling at high speed towards us.

"Cool it!" cried Louis, and the driver registered a mild complaint with me and then began to speed up again; diplomatic relations between the two had broken down days before.

All of us were wordless, though, when, out of nowhere, another white Toyota loomed behind us—and then, zigzagging wildly across the potholed road, roared straight ahead and disappeared, thick clouds of dust coming up to block our way as it accelerated off.

We kept on driving—what we had seen in Lalibela had shaken us out of easy words—and then, as we bumped over another pothole and came to the top of a small rise in the path, gears protesting, we saw a sight that rendered words irrelevant: the Toyota that had sped ahead of us twenty minutes before now sat motionless in a ditch. Its doors had been thrown open; two figures were slumped on its front seats.

"Stop!" cried Louis. "Stop the car!" I had no time to think, or fiddle around in my usual ineffectual way; already he was out, racing to the passenger side, where a foreign woman, older than we were, had been forced back against her seat by the collision.

He talked to her softly, asked her where it hurt, held her hand and told her it would be all right. Then he went round and attended to the driver, too.

"We've got to get them to a hospital," he shouted. This seemed a senseless wish: we were surrounded by hours of emptiness and those warnings about bandits were not far away. But Louis was as decisive as before he had been full of quips and neglected orders to the driver.

Very tenderly, he held the injured local man and helped him over to our vehicle, setting him up in the front seat, next to our driver, as if he were a precious statue. Then he brought the woman over—a motherly travel agent from Brooklyn, we learned, as humbled and out of it in this world of famine and rock churches as we were. He made room for her on one side of our seat, and he and I squeezed into the other.

We drove, slowly now, so as not to throw their bodies around and after a long, long while found the main road. Our driver stopped at a little line of shops and asked after a clinic and then—though the minutes were ticking by and our cargo was faltering—we found a hospital in the middle of the nowhereness. A gurney came out, another, and the two casualties disappeared from view, while we settled into chairs in a corridor and tried to distract ourselves.

Louis pulled out his backgammon set, but it didn't divert us as it had among the hill tribes of Chiang Mai. Great cries of pain emerged from the wards down the corridor, and then there was a silence that was no comfort at all. A bright-eyed young nurse walked past. "It's okay," she assured us. "Most of them are victims of gunshots. There is nothing to be done." The green walls were blotched with puddles of reddish brown, and there were bloodstains on the floor.

We sat and threw the dice; more howling came from the rooms. It might have been something from the book Louis read each day: the worship and prayer in the morning, the real life and suffering right now. They belonged together—neither had full meaning without the other—and I thought of all the stories that Louis had read, as the people around me had, about pain and what eases it in the long term.

Then a young doctor came out; remarkably, he spoke a little English. "Your friend," he said, "she's okay. She needs to rest, but she's been lucky."

"The driver?"

"Only bruises. They were fortunate."

They came out now—the American woman was smiling—and our driver asked directions to the nearest hotel. It was next to empty when we arrived, so we took over rooms, our plans forgotten, and, as we checked in, heard the woman ask if we would join her for dinner: she wanted to thank us for our help.

Two hours later, all three of us staggered down to a huge and almost empty lobby. At one table sat a glamorous young Indian woman with her boyfriend—both from London, we guessed from their voices in the near-silence. Otherwise, there was nothing.

We sat down, and our new friend began to talk about what she'd seen in Jerusalem, and her trip to Peru. The son et lumière in Egypt recently, and why she'd decided to come to Ethiopia to see if it might be a good spot for her clients. I noticed Louis looking around and realized he was restless and on his way to join the young couple at the next table; his Christian duty had been fulfilled, and now he was eager for adventure.

∴

A few days later, we were back in Addis, and the Christ-mas celebrations were coming to their peak. The next day Louis was due to fly back to London while I was on my way towards the Somali border, where there had been unrest, and then heading down to South Africa to witness the unraveling of apartheid. On his last night there, the whole broken city of creaking aid projects and shacks and hand-painted signs leading to dead-end roads or hotels that would perhaps never get built was filled with petitioners, all in white, streaming through the streets again, to chapels and churches and grave-yards. Night fell, and they lit tiny candles by which to guide themselves. We walked into a church and found it so full we could hardly move. People were chanting, their faces aglow, and boys were pounding on ox-skin drums. Bearded deacons and priests were reciting from illuminated books, and when we stepped out into the graveyard behind the church, there were bright faces lit by candles in every corner, then dozens more above what looked to be a manger, in new clusters com-ing in from the streets, soft high voices singing songs we didn't need Amharic to understand.

We walked around in a bit of a daze through much of the night; I don't think anything separated Louis the Christian from me the fascinated outsider. Everyone was brought into a circle of candles, and somehow the prayers and hymns made more sense in the light not only of the forlorn metropolis that otherwise was so dark after nightfall, but in the light of our long journey, and the caves in the high plateau and then the long afternoon in the hospital with the bloodstains.

I took Louis to the airport the next morning and returned to my little room in the Hotel Ghion, the voices of the night before, the shining, excited faces lit up by the candles, the accumulated sensations of the past few days, complex and contradictory, building and building inside me, when suddenly the phone began to shudder. "Iyer!" my friend was shouting over the scratchy line (last names were how we'd been taught to show closeness at school). "You'll never believe it! They took my cross away. The one I bought in Gondar. They say it has to be collected from some warehouse at the airport. Is there any way, do you think, you could . . ."

Go and collect it and give it to Giovanna, the stylish Italian travel agent who had set us up with our military driver.

I headed back to Bole International and found a huge hangar: sixteen centuries of confiscated crosses seemed to have been collected there, to gather dust. Things moved slowly anyway in this deeply impoverished country, and here I couldn't be sure that anything would ever stir. I sat against a wall in the drafty warehouse, and, now that Louis was gone, called upon my only other companion for the trip, Graham Greene. The last time I'd read *The End of the Affair,* I had been swept up in the story of passion and then, as so many other readers have been, felt stranded and confused by the notion of a man cuckolded by God. Now, with the chants going through me from the Christmas services, with my friend off to his first commitment, with the sight of the people walking across the high plateaus burning inside me, I began to understand how one could be transported—and left in the cold—by the spiritual surrender of another. God, if He exists, has to be something larger, more complex and mysterious than just a headmaster reading rules. Sometimes you know He exists, as with a love, only when He's very far away and you're shouting out your rage at Him.

∴

Farce and tragedy are separated by nothing but a trick of light: look at things one way and you can't stop laughing. Look at them in another and you feel completely helpless. A car crashes in an empty place and it could be the end of life; a good Samaritan comes to the rescue, as in an ancient parable, and the next thing you know, he's red-faced with drink and reenacting *Planes, Trains & Automobiles* for some bewildered kids from London.

What makes one weep and what makes one break out laughing are identical twins in Greene's work, and it sometimes seems almost a freak of fate, pure randomness, whether a character picks one or the other. Two telegrams are delivered in the wrong order—this had happened to Greene himself when his father died—and a message announcing a serious illness is delivered after the message announcing a death: is one's far-off father a Lazarus, or is life just playing a cosmic joke that can shatter one's heart?

A boy—another classically Greenian story—is summoned to his housemaster, who has difficult news to break: his father has been killed. By—as it happens—a falling pig. We know we shouldn't laugh, yet it's hard to summon the solemn tears the occasion calls for. We have to respond in some way, but we know that all our responses are likely to be the wrong ones.

Greene would always, with precise perversity, come at faith through the back door, not by way of the man of principle or pure saint, but through the confused bungler who inspires our pity and perhaps even our love with his fallenness. "The cruel come and go," as Wormold, the hapless main character in *Our Man in Havana* tells us, sadly, but the clown "was permanent." This ensured, perhaps, that the novelist would always feel much of the anguish of religion but little of its joy; it was rarely a pick-up to rally his spirits but always, if anything, a cause for remorse and a sense of unworthiness. It also meant that an act of conscience, even selflessness, on the part of a sinner invariably excited Greene more than (what most of us are excited to discover) an act of hypocrisy or folly in a priest or saint.

Yet every time I started to dwell on the agonized semi-Catholicism, and the man twisting and turning on his iron bed, I had to remember: many of his books were funny, wildly so, even as they rocked between moods—with their irregular system of chapters and sections—so you could never tell what was coming next. A cuckolded man (a dentist, of course) sits on a trick cushion, and it starts to play "Auld Lang Syne" as he weeps. A lonely man in Havana sends vacuum-cleaner designs to MI6 in London—he wants to earn enough money to buy his teenage daughter a horse—and when the designs are taken to be top-secret maps, innocents are killed on the basis of them. Sometimes Greene called his books "entertainments," but they were always shot through with a sense of sadness and being lost; the ones he called novels often had scenes of such riotous misunderstanding and knockabout poignancy that professors would refuse to take them seriously.

When he was stationed in West Africa during the war, by British intelligence, "Grim Grin" (as Kingsley Amis called him) came up with the idea of recruiting a French madam to set up a brothel at which he could pick up all the secrets of relaxing Vichy officers (the plan was almost adopted); whenever a London magazine ran a competition calling for parodies of Graham Greene, the man himself entered—and often won—then went on to incorporate the self-parodies in novels and memoirs. When, immediately after the war, he was working at a publishing house, Greene went to great trouble to make up a difficult author, Mrs. Montgomery, who started making furious calls to everyone on the staff, asking each in turn what had happened to her manuscript (he even used a friend to play the nonexistent writer on the phone). At one point he went so far as to take out an ad in *The Spectator* magazine from a make-believe biographer of Mrs. Montgomery (an allusion, perhaps, to the marginal character in Henry James's *Washington Square*?), and then wrote a letter from the imaginary Montgomery, in a subsequent issue, repudiating the biography.

It was as if, whenever the pressure began to build in him, pushing him towards a depression that ran so deep it could lead to thoughts of suicide, he tried to look for a burst of manic comedy to release him. Like many of us at our desks, he wrote his lightest books (*Our Man in Havana,* say) at a time when he was feeling defeated and battered by life, as if fiction could map out for him an alternate destiny. And his refusing to say, sometimes, whether his stories were sad or comical—his constant wavering between the two—came also from his sense, as he wrote in the Cuban novel, that "there was always another side to a joke, the side of the victim." He would amuse himself with a prank and then—the writer in him rising up—see the story from his target's point of view. I sometimes felt that Greene had created his version of God, as much as the other way round, so that he'd always have an external embodiment for his guilt and a reason to believe in justice, even if that meant his condemnation.

∴

There are often Henrys in the work of Henry Graham Greene—"A name I have always disliked," he later wrote—and they are nearly always mousy men, unnaturally passive, a little fearful of the world; they might almost stand for the part of their maker closest to his unworldly father, Charles Henry Greene, who once sent students off to see *Tarzan* because he thought it was an educational film. The nearest characters to Greene—or his other self—in the books tend always to be known, as in a British boys' school, by their last names, and these names sound as moldy and Anglo-Saxon as curses: Wormold, Bendrix, Fortnum, Fowler. Most of them grow movingly sympathetic as their stories go on, but still the world knows them and sees them only from afar, and the stress on their names falls always on the first syllable, so we're among "Worm," "Bend," "Fort" and "Fowl" (the women by their sides are always more tenderly and mellifluously seen—Milly, Sarah, Clara, Phuong).

Greene's main characters flinch from nicknames, as Greene did in life, and when the quiet American, in his innocence, tries to call Fowler "Tom," the older Englishman recoils at the unsought closeness, and says, "I'd rather you called me Thomas." That is, of course, the name of the disciple who doubted, and, through no coincidence, the name that Greene himself took on when being received into the church.

Greene told people that he turned to names like "Brown" and "Smith" and "Jones" because, when he chose, as a young writer, to give someone he'd met in Africa, in a nonfiction book, the more unusual name "Oakley," a real person called Oakley sued, won damages and forced the book out of print for several years. But that, like so much in him, seemed an intricate evasion. The effect of the anonymous names is to suggest grey and unloved Everymen wandering across an allegorical heath, like characters out of Beckett in their trash cans, though in these cases the wilderness is called Freetown or Port-au-Prince or Asunción. The books they inhabit stress always the human factor—five of his titles have "man" or "human" in them—and in two of the novels (*The Comedians* and *A Burnt-Out Case*) the protagonist is not even given a Christian name. Perhaps the most famous figure in all of Greene—the whisky priest we were made to read about at school—has no name at all.

"There is a strange importance about names," says Jim, the young boy at the center of Greene's last novel, *The Captain and the Enemy,* as he takes on the new name his adoptive parents have given him. It's an estimable sentiment—names are how we try to fix an identity and measure our closeness (or lack of it) to those around us—but the fact remains that Jim was once called "Victor." The charming crook who whisks him out of his school claims to have been born as "Brown," though at one point his friends call him "Roger" and elsewhere he goes by "Colonel Claridge." He signs checks as "Cardigan" or "Carver" and in Panama he passes as "Smith." At one point, he even signs a restaurant chit as "J. Victor (Capt.)," though shedding the name soon, if only because sympathy in Greene goes never to the victors and only to losers and the lost.

My first two names are the rather exotic and aspiring ones my father chose for me (that of the Buddha and the Neo-Platonist heretic); and my third and fourth names are, in fact, his, exactly, as if I were split down the middle—between his hopes for me and his inheritance to me, himself. He was wise enough to give me a global, European name, common to many languages, which would prove invaluable in an international life—easy to spell and to pronounce—and perhaps he intuited, too, that I would spend most of my life in a Buddhist country. When I write out all my initials and my name—the way I was known in school—it looks almost like a summons to sprightliness, or a boast.

Yet the fact that he was so charismatic has, almost inevitably, made me a little suspicious of charm, and determined to make myself neutral, private, ideally unseen; and the more I watched his fascination with magic, the more I tried to turn myself into a rationalist. Every son aspires to script an act 6 in a parent's life, and it's bound to veer off in a different, probably contrary direction. But every son is helpless before the lines on his palm.

"Look," said a Japanese matron who had installed herself on a landing in a Vancouver megabookstore, offering a free handwriting analysis to anyone who scribbled some words on a page.

"What's that?" I said, as she pointed towards the bottom of the page on which I'd written a few specimen sentences. She'd already unnerved me by identifying attentiveness, frugality, and even seeming contradictions—"This shows optimism," she said, motioning towards the slant of my script, "and this a wariness about the future," gesturing at my right-hand margins—that many a longtime friend might never quite see.

"You tell me."

"But isn't that your job?"

"No," she said. "It's nothing mystical. Just look."

She was right. The first name was so much larger than the second in my signature that it looked as if I was trying to define myself by myself, and not by my family. Even though, of course, both came from exactly the same place.

CHAPTER 7

A s I fell deeper—and deeper—into my Greene
thoughts, in a Greene shade, I noticed Hiroko looking at me strangely. She has a wonderful, bracing
lack of interest in all the things complicated men dream up
at their desks and a complete indifference to—an innocence
of—the stuff that people chatter about in the literary circles
of London or New York. When I heard critics drone on about
how Phuong in *The Quiet American* was "objectified," or two-
dimensional, the product of a man's boyish fantasy, I wondered how they could speak so coldly about the mysteries of
human kindness and affection. A companion is someone who
refuses to take the things we fret about too seriously—starting
with ourselves—even though she cares for us entirely. Phuong
offers the unquiet Englishman exactly the sense of peace and
acceptance he longs for—and cannot find—in church.

"You really want to spend all this time with Graham
Greene?" Hiroko asked.

"I suppose so. It's a way of working things out, as I couldn't
otherwise."

"*Otonoashii Amerikajin?*" she asked, incredulous; I'd foisted *The Quiet American* in Japanese on her years before.

"Well, not only that."

My life at my desk, my silly scribbles, were as strange to her as her job, selling clothes, was to me.

"You're going to write about his life?"

"Not exactly. About my life. Or how we project onto others . . ."

And then I stopped, because she deserved something better.

"Like His Holiness?"

"Well, a little bit like the Dalai Lama. He does teach me about kindness."

"You need hope in a book," she said, as she went out. "You won't forget toilet paper from the supermarket?"

∴

As soon as I met Carlos, on the streets of Havana, I could tell that he was a hustler of sorts. "Interesting," he said, as he saw me looking at a Space Age building along La Rampa, and I turned around; what was most interesting to me was that he spoke English, as few people did in Cuba in 1987. He had crinkly, strangely Chinese eyes and an ambiguous smile; his white shirt hung out from his trousers, and he might have been the kind of dissident who sidled up to foreigners on the streets of Prague or even Madrid. That I was a foreigner was evident from the fascination with which I was staring at a construction that must have looked like the future many years before; the only people who were transfixed by Cuba's future were the ones with the freedom to fly away from it.

"Come," he said, "I'll show you something more interesting," and he led me into a bus and downtown, to a dusty, high-ceilinged apartment, up a creaking, sweeping staircase, which might have belonged to Miss Havisham if she'd gone to serve her country in the tropics. There was a large, smiling black boy there, whom Carlos introduced, implausibly, as his brother; there were two girls, bubbly and unguarded, hanging their underwear to dry on the balcony. Though I'd arrived on the island only the night before, already I could feel the charm and sadness that lay in the "slow erosion" that Greene had described so hauntingly in Havana twenty-nine years before.

"So," Carlos said, as we left the others behind and went to a shiny (by Cuban standards) restaurant, where only foreigners (and their guests) could eat, and took our place in the long, long line gathered under the sun in the street. "How about you give me your passport? I fly to the Estados Unidos. You go to the American Interests Section on the Malecón and get a new one. I go to New York. I help you when I get there. Everybody wins."

"I see the logic of it," I said, "but let's wait a bit." I'd known the man only two hours and I could tell already that need was so advanced in Cuba that it infected every transaction.

"O-ka," he said, and for the next week Carlos was as good as his word. He never mentioned any such exchange again, and he took me everywhere I could want to see, offering a wry and literate and warm unofficial narration to what was not acknowledged in the huge billboards shouting "*Venceremos!*" or "*Patria o Muerte.*" He invited me to stay in his apartment, if I liked, where kids were catching the AM stations from Miami, while a rooster clucked around and out onto the adjacent rooftop (the bird was called "Reagan," Carlos said, because he never stopped squawking). He pulled out books from his shelves—Spinoza, Saroyan—and asked me what I thought of them. He slipped me into nightclubs that were open only to those who knew how to knock on the door in the right way; he offered me girls, cigars, anything I might need.

"My dream," he said, "when I get out, is to make a library. In New York City. Where people can drink coffee and read books."

"A library?"

"No, sorry. A 'bookstore.' A bookstore café where people can talk about anything. In freedom."

When I flew back to California and asked him what I could send him—anything at all—he asked only for an American flag and a recording of "The Star-Spangled Banner."

I'd met Carlos many times already in my twenty-nine years; the previous fall, in the little town of León, in Nicaragua, I'd passed a friendly young woman on the street and she'd caught my eye and smiled. Within five minutes, she'd asked me (then and there, on the street) if I'd marry her. I smiled, but she was serious; she wanted to escape, and if I could give her what she wanted, she could give me something, too.

In Burma, two years before, I'd met a sweet-natured young character who hung around the fanciest hotel, the then-derelict Strand, and who remembered having met me there two years earlier; he became my shadow guide to the city, telling me what his closed country was like under the surface as I told him what America and Britain were like, beyond the rumors that he'd heard of them. In difficult or impoverished countries, the leap of faith becomes instantly human, and very personal, as in every Greene novel I'd loved: How much do you trust this stranger who seems so ready to be your friend? How much does he—or should he—trust you?

Like many who had been to the island, among them Greene, of course (and the Greenian Trappist, Thomas Merton), I fell quickly in love with the complications of Cuba, and the day after I returned to California following my first trip, I went to a travel agent and bought a ticket to go back, three months later. I had never seen a place so stirring in its passions and so constant in its doubts and rumors; Cuba was like a furious, never-ending debate on whom and what to believe, which words to trust, whether to enjoy the warm wind coming off the water along the seaside road, with its fading, rainbow-colored buildings—or the desperate kids gathered on the rocks below, trying to slip away.

I'd never met such resilient, spirited, often irresistible people, but the result was that the whole country seemed a kind of hotheaded family that had been cooped up in the same quarters for much too long.

The strict father bolted the doors, his daughter tried to slip out through a second-floor window, his son shouted constant imprecations at him and the tearful, desperate mother sobbed and clutched at the elbows of all the other three, asking them to settle down, while she took silent notes to report on her loved ones to her sister.

∴

When I flew back for my second trip—to coincide with the celebrations for the twenty-ninth anniversary of the Revolution and Carnival—Carlos was waiting for me at the airport, ready to take me to Santiago or Artemisa or the home of Lourdes, who had so liked me, he said, when we met before (but to whom, I knew, I could never give the freedom and escape that she needed). "The man I remembered might have been a swindler," I recalled having read in Greene's account of Cuba in his memoirs, "but he had been a good guide to the shadier parts of Havana, and I had no desire for a dull and honest man to be my daily companion on this long trip." I knew Carlos had something to gain from me—almost the only foreigners to be seen in Havana in 1987, other than Russians, were pasty-faced Bulgarians, emptying the tinned peaches in the breakfast rooms of ghostly hotels, and North Koreans walking in pairs, with a small badge depicting the "Great Leader" next to their hearts.

But I had something to gain from him, too, and we'd have become friends in any circumstances. He was quick-witted, deeply cultured, kind; his hunger to learn about the United States, the place where he might be able to make a new life, seemed perfectly to match my hunger to learn about how the Revolution really felt to its so-called beneficiaries, at some level deeper than mere politics. Some people who'd never been to Cuba called it a socialist paradise; the U.S. government, under Reagan, was convinced it was a totalitarian hell. Neither began to correspond to the quicksilver, open, ardent and suspicious place I saw, which reminded me daily, as Greene would have said, that in matters of love and family, there are no easy answers or unmixed emotions.

After I got home from my second trip, Carlos kept on sending me letters, reporting on the many ways he was trying to make his escape: he had "married," he said, a woman he'd been married to before, because her father had fought with Fidel and might look out for him. He was going now to the Peruvian embassy to seek amnesty, and he was hoping to use thousands of dollars to get a fake passport from the Dominican Republic. He'd been in prison once, so there was a chance he could come out legally, as a political refugee; he needed my help with the authorities in Washington.

I'd been through versions of the same story time and again—it sometimes seemed the story of my life—but never had I felt so close to the situation that is at the center of most Greene books: two men come together in the dark and open their hearts as they can, perhaps, only with strangers, forming a bond, even as they know little of each other. It's often the closest thing to faith as exists in the work. It wasn't just trivial correspondences, I was coming to see, that made me feel close to the English novelist, the way we'd met similar people, or both found an air of bungled secrecy and cruel misunderstandings on the backstreets of Santiago; it was that he was giving me a searchlight to understand how Carlos, in his life of rumor and drama, was leading an existence that I could hardly imagine, and how my life of relative peace seemed fantasy to him. The comedian, as Greene would have it, always gets implicated in the end.

∴

At last word came through that Carlos had indeed gotten out, as a former inmate of Castro's prisons, and now I began to receive calls from him, in his temporary home in New York's Hell's Kitchen. I happened to be flying back to the city a little later, and we met in Times Square, the place he'd dreamed of all his life, and went for a celebratory meal at Victor's, the Cuban restaurant on Fifty-second Street.

"We're only a few blocks away from the office where I first

wrote about you," I told him, gesturing at the Time-Life Building, on Fiftieth. He toasted us and ordered more roast pork and declared that now, for the first time ever, his future could be what he wanted.

But life is difficult for newcomers to the Land of the Free from a very different system; Carlos soon ended up in New Jersey, and then headed down to Florida, the very place he'd told me he never wanted to go ("Too much like Cuba"). He wrote to me constantly, and we spoke often on the phone—it had rarely been possible before—and when I flew down to Havana again, for my sixth visit, he suggested we meet up, on the way, in Miami.

He was staying in a beat-up motel, I gathered, though he made sure that I didn't see it; he insisted on putting me up (at his expense) in a top-floor suite in the smallish hotel where he was working now. We were happy to meet again; it felt as if we'd been through several lifetimes together. But there was no talk of a bookstore café now, I noticed. The future had seemed illimitable in Cuba, so long as it had not been something real.

"You hear from Peter and Lourdes?" he asked me.

"Now and then. I'll see them this week when I'm back in Havana." (Peter, though, was in prison now, and when I went to visit him there, exulted in the fact that he had three solid meals a day, a steady roof above his head, all the things he could not be sure of on the outside.)

Carlos took me to a mall, the very brightest and splashiest, I could imagine, in South Florida. We stood outside the entrance to a theme-park café. It was a long line, and we both thought of the long line we'd been standing in our first morning together, when he'd asked me for my passport, so he could enjoy a piece of my life.

"You know, I write to Peter and Lourdes," he now said. "I talk to them on the telephone sometimes. I tell them, 'Is better where you are. For me is okay here. I can hustle.'" The crinkly eyes had not changed at all. "But for them is better in La Habana. No work, but no hassle. No future but no schedule."

"Death by gunshot or death by starvation," I said, reminding him of what an old man in Santiago had said to us about the difference between life under Batista and life under Fidel.

He smiled, in recognition. Greene had been ignorant, by his own admission, of some of the brutalities that were taking place behind the devil-may-care atmosphere he so enjoyed, and when he went back to Cuba and became a friend of Fidel's, he seemed almost perversely eager to champion the place as a way of tweaking the newly dominant world power in Washington. "There is a touch of ancient Athens about Havana today," he'd written in London's *Sunday Telegraph*, after a trip in 1963. "The Republic is small enough for the people to meet in the agora." It was often suspected that he was reporting on the island for MI6, and that maybe even his support of the Revolution was a front.

But beneath all the geopolitical ironies, and the ways he'd chosen to turn the place into a free-and-easy escape of sex shows and bordellos, Greene had given me something deeper, which now I couldn't shake off. We had dinner at the theme-park café, and we talked about everything but the future—or the present. When I looked at Carlos, I tried not to say all the things that were coming to both our minds, as he smiled, ambiguously as ever, and asked me if I wanted dessert.

CHAPTER 8

Often, as the years went on, I told myself I'd had enough of Greene. I never wanted to hear another word from him or about him. I had no interest in encountering again his close readings of *The Tale of the Flopsy Bunnies* or reading how *The Roly-Poly Pudding*, by Beatrix Potter, is a "masterpiece," by an author comparable to Henry James. I grew tired of his self-conscious talk of Russian roulette and suicide, though I could believe—since it came out so often in his work—that he frequently did see death as a release or a liberation. I wasn't sure even the younger Greene would have liked the scold of later years, lecturing the press on Central America—although my travels there had shown me he was right—and I found it hard to get inside his frequent melancholy. The "honesty" with which Greene insisted on telling his women about the other women in his life sounded like pure selfishness; the confessor is determined to get his betrayals off his chest, even if that means just foisting them on someone else.

He was like any friend, in short, with whom one's spent a lot

101

of time; I thought of Louis's eagerness to run away from the good deed he'd so instinctively performed in Ethiopia, though that did nothing to diminish the goodness or the deed. Greene was the opposite of a holy book, by his own admission; he was a human book, in whose novels the characters act well only in spite of themselves, and after a long series of self-betrayals. I knew the paradoxical truth he was getting at—"If only you'd forget your guilt," his wife used to say to him, "you'd treat me more nicely"—but I couldn't bear reading the early stories, so bitter and cruel and thick with dissatisfaction. And his travel books were a near-perfect example of how not to write or think about travel.

∴

Pick up *The Lawless Roads,* Greene's account of wandering through Mexico, in fact, and you will never want to pick him up again. It's hard to imagine any work about a journey abroad—the completion of a trip that the author has planned and looked forward to for two and a half years—so dyspeptic, so loveless, so savagely self-enclosed and blind. "Hate" is the word that resounds throughout, as in much of the early work, like an inverted "Amen." Within a day or two of arriving in Mexico, Greene declares, "That, I think, was the day I began to hate the Mexicans." Many pages later, he is still intoning, "I have never been in a country where you are more aware all the time of hate."

The book might almost be a parody not just of Graham Greene, but of the kind of Englishman who hates Abroad the minute he sets foot in it, yet punishes himself—and the rest of us—by choosing to go there again and again. A child in Mexico is "odious." Mexicans are "like mangy animals in a neglected zoo" observing "the jungle law." By the time the trip, which lasted less than two months, is coming to an end, Greene is confidently asserting, "It is not inconceivable that the worst evil possible to natural man may be found years hence in Mexico."

"The whole atmosphere of the place is rotten." "Lunch was awful, like the food you eat in a dream, tasteless in a positive way, so that the very absence of taste is repellent." A market is "far more squalid than anything I had seen in the West African bush." Sex is the "deed of darkness" and when he records a "silly dream," it is one of "triumph and happiness."

Every now and then the thirty-three-year-old Englishman does catch a glimpse of simplicity and peace, as of life before the fall, but this only makes the rest of his days more terrible. "One did want, I found, an *English* book in this hating and hateful country," he writes, and decides to pick up Cobbett and Trollope as he's passing through some of the most spectacular scenery he could have encountered in his young life. He is developing, he notes, "an almost pathological hatred" for Mexico. As he nears the end of the trip, as if impervious to all he's been saying and thinking, he writes, "How one begins"— begins!—"to hate these people."

A few months after completing the nightmare journey— England, when he returns, is so miserable, he wonders how he could have hated Mexico—Greene wrote a novel, arising out of one stray detail he'd picked up on his journey: a story of a drunken priest so feckless that he'd christened a boy "Brigitta." In *The Lawless Roads* the tale is merely one more instance of Mexican clumsiness and folly, another reason to hold the malfunctioning country in contempt. In the novel, however, *The*

Power and the Glory, the tiny anecdote becomes the foundation for a devastating, heartfelt story of a priest who violates every rule of the church and yet can never quite manage to betray its spirit.

The novel was so full of compassion and fellow feeling for the man—indeed, for all the luckless and broken figures in the Mexican landscape (not least the lieutenant in pursuit of the priest)—that it became the book that established Greene as a major writer on religion and remained the one novel even its contentious maker admitted to liking through most of his life. When Catholicism was on the run, he'd side even with the Catholics. When a priest was a fallen, sinning man much like the rest of us, Greene could summon sympathy even for a priest. All that was so hateful and bereft of light and beauty to the traveler, watching from the sidelines, becomes moving and deeply personal for the novelist, as soon as he sees and feels from within an abandoned little girl and the fugitive who's been trying for ten years to run away from what he loves.

∴

That Greene should find hate everywhere in Mexico was off-putting enough; but that Greene should sense that this hate was really in himself was even more harrowing, especially for an admirer. He was a professional writer of fiction, yet Greene was never one to lie to himself, I felt, despite those two versions of his diary. That was what commanded respect even when I couldn't give him affection; he looked unblinkingly at precisely the shadows in the self (and in the world) that most of us try to look away from, drilling, as a dentist might, into the most tender and infected spaces because that was where the trouble lay. That was what allowed so many to write so venomously about Greene; he gave them all the evidence they needed in his compendious accounts of what he called his "evasions and deceits."

There is a moment in *The Lawless Roads* that stuck with me every time I read it. Greene goes to Villahermosa—or "Beautiful City," as it would be in English—and in the midst of what looks as if it might almost be redeeming, he catches sight of a dentist's office, with its "floodlit chair of torture." As if caught in some nightmare in which he can't escape himself, he is told, improbably, "Why, everybody in Villahermosa is called Greene—or Graham." Two pages later, "a young Mexican dentist called Graham joined us." As he leaves Villahermosa, Greene goes into the depths of the jungle, where (of course) his landlord is "dumb with misery—he had toothache."

It is as if he is trapped in a hall of mirrors, and every road he travels brings him back to his own pain. He is lost, raging, inside his own head. One can feel the anguish of such a situation—but that makes it no easier to like the man who's going through it.

I thought again of his early stories set in England, so full of places called "Fetter Lane" and "Leadenhall Street"— "Wotton-under-Edge"—and the overwhelming impression was of a man imprisoned, in a cell that he has committed himself to of his own free will. He has given himself to a marriage, though he knows that he can never settle down; pledged himself to a faith, though his captious mind refuses to believe in anything but uncertainty; and put himself inside a family though nothing makes him feel less at home. The medicine he's taken is the one that makes him ill—and the only person he can blame for all his suffering is himself.

In his early novel *Stamboul Train* (the one that helped

make him truly independent, after it was bought by Hollywood), every character on the eponymous train is a fugitive
and a solitary of sorts, and the very carriages that might seem
vessels of freedom become vehicles of imprisonment. But the
worst of the itinerant figures is a thief and adulterer who is
even, we are made to guess, guilty of murder. Greene gives
him, a little implausibly, the name "Grünlich," which in German, of course, means "greenish."

And yet *The Power and the Glory*, arising out of the trip
he so claimed to hate, seemed to release Greene a little: from
Britain, from his sense of enclosure, from self-division. There
is more daylight, even sunshine in the books that follow—the
Mexican novel is the first with no Englishman at the center and with a vivid habitation of a foreign landscape—and
though there is always contention at their heart, it is sweet-
ened, sometimes soothed by the passions of a foreign country,
as the writer's alter ego tries to bring his loves in tune with
the complex environment around him. In time he would step
beyond even those tensions and give us the gentler landscape
of friendship (in *Monsignor Quixote*) or of a too-innocent man
being introduced to the follies of moralism by a woman (*Travels with My Aunt*). The country he claimed to hate would turn
him towards love.

∴

If you look at Greene's private life, it's easy to believe that
you're reading a kind of cautionary tale fashioned by some
malign allegorist. The woman he married, Vivienne (later
Vivien) Dayrell-Browning, bore a family name that showed
her connection to the Victorian poet Greene always loved,

the slippery hymnist of doubt and desire who'd written, "Our interest's on the dangerous edge of things. / The honest thief, the tender murderer, / The superstitious atheist." Yet at the same time she was a deeply devout nineteen-year-old convert to Catholicism who had contacted him when she read an article he'd written in an Oxford undergraduate magazine on how people were "considerably oversexed"; you couldn't, she advised him, use the word "worship" in the context of the Virgin Mary (the correct term was "hyperdulia").

Vivien would become, of all improbable things, an expert on doll's houses, who found herself married to what she later called "the wildest of creatures, and the least domesticated." She put a crib in the family dining room every Christmas so that the Holy Child could sit in the middle of the household, even as her husband was in perpetual flight from any reminder of sanctity and fidelity. When Greene joined the Church in order to marry his shy young bride, then working for the Oxford publishers Blackwell's, he was prepared for conversion by a "Father Trollope" who had been an actor on the London stage.

In later years he would move in the opposite direction; his strongest loves were a Swedish actress, Anita Björk; his longtime American mistress, Catherine Walston; and the married Frenchwoman he met in Africa who would share his final thirty-two years with him, Yvonne Cloetta. Walston had approached him as a stranger—the heavy hand of bad drama intrudes again, as he might have put it—because she'd decided to become a Catholic, she said, after reading his books; she wanted to know if he'd be her godfather. He was happy to say yes, but, since he was busy at the time of her ceremony, he asked Vivien to go in his stead. Later it would be rumored that he and Walston read theology in bed and made love behind every other high altar in Italy. She incited his jealousy—which he could never distinguish from love—by flirting with priests in particular, one of whom had authored a book called *Morals and Marriage: The Catholic Background to Sex.*

At the moment Catherine entered his life, in 1946, he had been spending much of his time for the past eight years with another mistress, Dorothy Glover. She was—unusually for Greene—English, unmarried and not physically command-ing, according to his friends. But they'd grown close in the Blitz, when London had seemed almost a foreign city, alight with drama, and they'd made love in public air-raid shelters, while choosing to remain in the middle of the conflagration, on fire watch. Greene wrote (anonymously, at first) the texts to books called *The Little Train, The Little Fire Engine, The Little Horse Bus* and *The Little Steamroller* so that Dorothy's illustrations to these stories could be published. When she died, in 1971, Greene wept bitterly, Yvonne Cloetta writes in her memoirs, for almost the only time in their more than three decades together.

∴

I never felt myself," wrote the Englishman always on the move, "till I had put at least the Channel between my native country and me"; he seemed desperate, throughout his adult life, to be away from the cocktail parties and literary conver-sations he knew too well in London. He haunted the opium dens of the Far East and visited Tahiti, where dramas were less predictable; he stayed in Capri, wondering "who I am," and everywhere he went, he collected expats, lonely men and renegade priests who'd made a kind of life abroad. Finally he settled in the south of France and wrote something called *The Tenth Man.*

His travels seemed to awaken in him an ineradicable sense of mystery; if he did not really believe in God, he wrote, he always had a keen sense of the devil. Much of his life, in fact, he saw as a spirited argument with God: "I should have thought that it was God who had cause to be humble," he wrote, "when he reflects upon what an indifferent mess he has made in the creation of a human being." He had a special symbol stitched into the cover of all his books—he was always fascinated by spells—to protect him from the evil eye, and in one early novel, a character bargains with God, having "conceived the notion that if she promised God to give him up, God would spare him."

Yet at the same time, he had no patience with missionaries or sermonizers, anyone who would lay down a simple law of right and wrong; his travels, his very novelist's intuition, gave him a supple appreciation of how much in each of us lies beyond the grasp of reason. He was never a joiner, and it was boredom that seemed to propel him away from Mayfair; his countrymen mocked him for his readiness to help prostitutes—he had a soft spot for the fallen—and his problem, he was shrewd enough to see, was that he had a gift for getting involved with the wrong woman and then lacking the courage to break off the connection.

He was always too popular and readable to win much critical acclaim; Hollywood continues to make films out of even his lesser works, and suspicion attaches to him because of all the work he did for British intelligence (he wrote spy novels as well as exotic entertainments). Though clearly romantic, and full of a gentleman's often fatal sense of chivalry, he never denied the "essential aloofness" that the writer's job demands and sensed that his soft heart would always get him in deeper trouble than his cool mind. He recoiled from a formal divorce from his wife because, as he said, no woman would ever take pity on a weak man. "Pity" itself he saw as a great affliction, a kind of weakness disguising itself as charity.

Yet perhaps the single most important thing to be said about him was that he was an undeluded, open, antimoralistic adventurer (his work was denounced by the Vatican) who wanted to see every situation in the round. "It would be silly," he wrote during the war, "to deny that our enemies have some of the same virtues as we; they have at least courage, loyalty and professionalism." He ended his days still in exile, looking back on his old boarding school and writing pieces like "The Three Fat Women of Antibes." From the outset he had been painfully aware (as only the innocent can be) that innocent intentions are the undoing of many a man: "In this world," a character says in a novel he wrote when he was barely thirty, "it's the good who do all the harm." Fascinated by goodness, he always had a complex, shifting sense that humanity lay far beyond our salvationist ideas. "Perhaps even the best of us are sinners," he wrote (too characteristically), "and the worst of us are saints."

Somerset Maugham, however—the "he" in every one of the above clauses, though nearly every one fits Greene—was so close to his successor in his worldly acuity, his hunger for the far-off place and his love of human waywardness and surprise that Greene claimed to have no affection for him. Maugham relied too much on the anecdote, he said, and lacked the inwardness, the nuance and the risk taking that marked out Greene's chosen literary mentor (and Maugham's anathema) Henry James; ultimately he put storytelling before psychology. Greene constantly stressed how little he owed to Maugham, the way some of us stress how different—how very different—we are from our fathers, the ones we've spent our lifetimes defining ourselves in opposition to; in much the same way, John le Carré, Greene's literary son, often got prickly when asked what he owed to the apostle of doubt who was, he once admitted, a "guiding star" to him when young.

Yet Greene read Maugham's *Ashenden* before embarking on *Our Man in Havana* (the clear model for le Carré's *Tailor of Panama*) and mocked romanticism and idealism as only a sometime romantic and idealist, like Maugham, could do. When V. S. Naipaul visited Greene in Antibes, he wrote that he could see through the window, down the coast, Maugham's huge villa in Cap Ferrat, mocking and contrasting in its splendor the functional anonymity of Greene's one-bedroom flat.

∴

How arbitrary such affinities are, I thought every time I returned to Maugham: why, in a country full of elegant women with silky dark hair, should I feel that Hiroko—and only Hiroko—was a person I could give myself to forever, a lost piece of myself? Why, when Maugham gave me stories of exploration and escape that I read and reread with such delight—"It may be that my heart, having found rest nowhere, had some deep ancestral craving for God and immortality which my reason would have no truck with"—did I feel that he was an author close to my heart, and yet Greene somehow a secret nestled within that heart, reflecting it back to me? Why did certain forgotten pathways in the eastern hills of Kyoto have the capacity to pierce me as none of the streets I knew in the Oxford of my birth or the Santa Barbara of my upbringing could ever do?

It was as if, underneath the self I knew and was in public, there was another self, mysterious even to its owner, that lived beyond the grasp of explanation but would read Greene's works as if they were a private diary, Maugham's as if they were only a brilliant fiction. And in the process—much like Greene, in fact, whenever he was asked about Maugham—bridle testily and throw out subterfuges whenever I was asked about the real person I resembled, the one with the wild hair exploding at the sides and the mischievous glint in the eye, whom I saw whenever I looked in the mirror.

CHAPTER 9

There were fires raging all across the hills around our house, and I was sitting in a downtown restaurant with my mother and Hiroko. I'd flown into Santa Barbara two days before, and, driving along the empty road that leads from the airport to our house ten minutes away, I'd looked up into the hills to where the lights of our home shine alone on our ridge, and my heart had stopped. There were two bright blazes of orange cutting through the darkness, with a speed and efficiency I remembered from the time when our home—in the same location—had burned down (with me beside it) some years before.

I accelerated wildly up the hill and started taking the curves along the mountain road leading up to our solitary house at a crazy speed. The air to the north was already red and full of smoke—infernal—and as I pushed the car to go faster, I saw sightseers along the side of the road gathering to watch the unearthly light show, great towers of orange, a hundred feet high, rising from the valleys just below our home and smoke turning the sky into a sickly pall.

I swerved, brakes screaming, into our driveway, and summoned my wife and mother out to see what was happening a mile or two away. It looked to be remote still, but I remembered how, during the previous fire, the flames had raced through the brush at seventy miles an hour, so that an orange gash in what looked to be a distant slope was suddenly a pillar of flames arcing over our living-room windows.

The next day we awoke to the sound of helicopters whirring overhead. The sky was a grisly blood-red color. The house felt hot already, and, although the smoke seemed to clear as the wind shifted and returned us to a placid blue midsummer day, as the afternoon went on the sky above the ridge next to us turned a hideous, end-of-the-world color, or discolor really, ash falling around us like snow.

I went with Hiroko down to the post office, and as we came out, after a short transaction, the whole suburb around us was black with coughy smoke. We looked up to the hills, to where our house and our far-off neighbors were, and all we could see were one, two, three slashes of orange angrily starting up across the slopes. We began to drive home and, switching on the radio, I heard that our house and the few up the road had been issued an "evacuation warning." I turned into our little road and began driving up it, and the announcer on the local radio, frantic, said that the "evacuation warning" had been turned into an "order": we had to leave now, or we would be forced out.

We drove the remaining five minutes at a crazy speed again, collected my mother, her dazed cat inside a little cage, gathered as many precious papers and photos as we could in five minutes and then tore down the road again, fire trucks coming past us in the opposite direction, plumes of smoke seeming to rise from all the valleys and the crevices in the hills, the air so thick we were choking already and driving out of what seemed to be an oven, the huge flames cresting above our house as if ready to engulf it.

Now, barely twenty minutes away, downtown Santa Barbara was dreaming through another placid blue-sky afternoon, a miracle of calm; the angry smoke and orange burns to the north seemed to belong to another universe. We had to go about our life as usual—the next day would bring a fireworks display along the beach, for July the Fourth, and the day after that, I was due to perform a wedding ceremony for a college friend who was flying over from England for the occasion. We needed dinner, preferably in some inexpensive place not far from the house where we were staying while technically homeless (the same building that had housed my mother and me for four months after our house burned down before).

"There's a story of the Buddha," my mother began telling us now, perhaps to take our mind off the conflagration, and I listened to her, though usually all the wisdom that came from her, a teacher of comparative religions, I tried to block out because I was a son. "When his closest disciple, Ananda, asked him what was the greatest miracle," she went on, "walking on water or conjuring jewels out of thin air, changing the heat of one's body through meditation or sitting undisturbed in a cave for years and years, he said, 'Simply touching the heart of another human being. Acting kindly. That's the greatest miracle of all.'"

"The church of humanity, in other words," I said, "like Graham Greene." I didn't care that I was citing the very writer my mother had liked when I was at school and I had mocked. ("You remember," she said, not unexpectedly, "who it was who told you to read Graham Greene?"). "It was what he always believed in, the human predicament, the possibility for kindness and honesty even in the midst of our confusions and our sins. He could never quite bring himself to believe in God; God was the Other with whom he played his incessant games of 'He loves me, He loves me not.' But in humanity he had the strongest, if most reluctant belief. In our fallenness lies our salvation."

The other two looked at me blankly, nonplussed by this explosion. "He never could have much confidence in faith and hope," I said, concluding a sermon that no one had asked for. "But charity was the one thing he couldn't turn away from. Many writers try to take a journey into the Other. But in him it becomes a kind of creed, his version of religion, even when he's just traveling into the Other in himself."

What I really could have been saying was that we were now in the world he'd made so real to me in his books, at the mercy of much larger forces, pushed back to essentials, without a home. The only thing you could possibly do in such circumstances was see that so many others were in a similar predicament and reach out towards them; what you shared was not faith, usually, but unsettledness.

Up in the hills, meanwhile, the fires continued to blaze.

∴

He was very sweet and modest," said his friend and contemporary Evelyn Waugh, of Greene, though Waugh was never given to syrupy or benign pronouncements, "always judging people by kindness." He had agreed to look at a much-rejected manuscript called *Swami and Friends* in 1935, and gone to the trouble of finding a publisher for it, and become a staunch champion and finally a friend of its previously unknown writer, R. K. Narayan (born Rasipuram Krishnaswami Narayanaswami Iyer, I later learned, the only member of our extended clan to have won a name for himself in English letters). In judging him unworthy of a Nobel Prize in 1950, Per Hallström, a member of the Nobel committee, had written that compassion in Greene is "the only way to achieve human kind's and life's inner meaning," more or less the center of his religion. But Greene was reluctant, almost ashamed, to be seen being kind; it was only at his memorial service that Muriel Spark revealed that he had sent her a little money every month so that she could go on writing—accompanied by some bottles of red wine, so she wouldn't feel like a charity case.

Greene often took up irrational hatreds in his life and never missed a chance to plague do-gooders and moralists; whenever I met someone who knew him well, the word that came up, in the midst of admiration, was "difficult." With a tendency, as more than one acquaintance noted, to need to make conflict out of peace, as if to answer to some turmoil inside himself, he was so brutal on the unmet Noël Coward that Coward sent him a plaintive letter in verse, asking him what he'd done to deserve it (find success and avoid heavy-handedness?). He seemed to feast on confrontations, perverse or paradoxical positions, as if he would take any stance so long as it kept him apart from the crowd.

But if his books have one signal quality, it is compassion— the fellow feeling that one wounded, lonely, scared mortal feels for another, and the way that sometimes, especially in a moment of crisis, when we "forget ourselves" (which is to say, escape our thoughts and conscious reflexes), a single extended hand makes nonsense of all the curlicues in our head. It can even make our terrors go away, for a moment.

"It's not really an established church or creed," I might have said, if my mother and Hiroko had not saved me over my pasta from myself. "He was an apostle in a church of one. But what he was laying down, in effect, was a code of right action. Not faith, or God, or even justice—in none of which he can really believe; just the possibility of a single decent action. For no reason at all."

∴

The next day, when Hiroko and my mother and I woke up in a strange house, in downtown Santa Barbara—odd to think we'd thought, in coming back here from Japan, that we could help my mother—I walked out into the parking lot to see what I could make out in the distance, where our house had been. The skies were black. It was as if a curtain had come down to separate us from whatever the rising fires were doing a few miles to the north. On the news, as ever, the reports said that the fire was less than twenty percent contained; hundreds of firefighters were being called in from across the country, and the governor had declared a state of emergency. The previous year, two miles from our house, the second largest fire in California history had wiped out 240,000 acres of land. The roof of my aging green Toyota was still splotched with permanent brown bruises from the ash.

We were stuck now in this halfway house, unable to return home; calls, e-mails were coming in from friends: "We just saw the map on the Internet. It looks as if the fires are a few hundred yards from your house." "We heard on the news that they have a fire truck stationed next to every house on your road. It can't happen again, can it? Twice in less than twenty years."

We needed to get away from this, I thought—all the human chatter, and anguish over what we could do nothing about—so I got into the little car, with Hiroko by my side, and we drove up to a monastery in the hills a few minutes away, several ridges south of our house, where often I went to collect myself, and to gain clarity and direction. It was in this same place, in fact, that I'd decided to pursue Graham Greene the previous month, though all sense and logic (like the contracts I'd signed) said I was meant to be addressing the much more attractive theme of Japan's changing surfaces and life as a happily bewildered foreigner.

We drove up past the old Spanish mission, one of the most beautiful churches in California, with a convent next to its garden and courtyard, and took the steep road up along the hills, past the local reservoir, and then to the great open space that leads to hidden Mount Calvary. I'd discovered the place only a few years before, after thirty-five years in Santa Barbara; it had become my secret home, to be used whenever I could not visit the monastery three hours up the coastal road to the north, in the stretch of coastline called Big Sur, where I'd begun to stay seventeen years before.

Now, though, that monastery to the north was surrounded by flames, too; twenty-six structures in the area were gone, and the fire had been blazing there for almost two weeks. In Colombia one morning, the previous week, I'd received an e-mail from a nun friend saying that the hermitage we both loved was going up in flames, and I should pray for it, and our common friends there.

Today, ironically, the firefighters protecting my beloved sanctuary in Big Sur were being summoned down to Santa Barbara to protect our house and the ones around it. It was like some parable in which all the escape lanes in one's head are blocked; wherever one turns, there's a wall of fire.

We got out of the car at the top of the mountain, after following the narrow, empty road up through the hills and then turning into a tiny entrance that snaked around the dry brush for a few quiet seconds to the Santa Barbara retreat house. The air pulsed with silence around us. We could feel the stillness, the clarity in a place like this, as if murmured prayers, over years, unending, had polished the silence till it shone, the way workers in fancy hotels polish the windows and the wooden floors.

I followed Hiroko in through the main entrance, and we walked into a little sunlit courtyard. Sitting there, in a circle of light, in the silence, yellow and orange flowers along the borders, a makeshift crucifix in front of us, with skulls around it, we said nothing, letting the gathered tension of the last few days come out of us. There was a wooden bench, with a small plaque remembering a donor who had passed; we might have been in sixteenth-century Spain, a place where fires in Santa Barbara had never been heard of and people lived their lives according to a calendar that had no dates.

"Remember the last time we came here?" I asked her.

"Two years ago?" (She remembers everything, keeping me honest.) "When you were going to Sri Lanka?"

"Right. I don't know why, but I felt I needed blessings then, protection. I don't even know if I believe in gods, but this was the only place to come to."

"It's okay," she said, though forty-eight hours earlier, fleeing the burning hills, she'd broken into uncharacteristic tears. "Everything will be fine."

Just sitting in the silent courtyard made everything fall away. The days, our cares, the fact that we were staying in a house not our own, our belongings engulfed. The silence seemed to be a sifting mechanism, so that everything trivial and divisive disappeared—the setting, too—and all that remained was what was clear and impossible to argue away.

"You feel better?" I asked Hiroko, after perhaps thirty minutes.

"It's calm." Which wasn't exactly a yes.

"Shall we go?" Just a short time collecting ourselves— recollecting ourselves—in such a place made all the difference; now whatever came at us over the radio, from thoughtful friends, from the furnace of our minds would have a frame around it, a background of unchangingness to set against it.

As we walked out of the main building, letting the heavy door close behind us, and walked towards my car, the unsightly puddles of corroded brown on its green roof recalling the fire of the summer before, I looked over along the hills to where I didn't even expect to see our house. There it was, to my amazement, a tiny structure from this distance, impossibly frail, by itself on the ridge, huge plumes of smoke rising all around it. Then the thick black clouds descended once again, and I was sure that it was gone.

∴

The world of Greene is a world of greys, I thought, back in our temporary quarters—which is to say, the world of our conflicting emotions. It is not that good and bad do not exist, but that they are so improbably mixed, in constantly shifting proportions, that we cannot begin to tell friend from foe or right from wrong; the priest is likely to be a reprobate and the sinner to have some residual kindness in him. The God we believe in dispenses suffering—and the devil promises us happiness, or peace. The quiet American is a fool because he wishes to lay down theories and systems on what is as impossible to predict or control as a forest fire; the unquiet Englishman is a fool because to give up on hope and caring is to commit oneself prematurely to a kind of death-in-life. Vienna's main sewer—in the classic film Greene wrote, *The Third Man*—flows straight into the Danube.

He was part of the first generation to grow up with the cinema—he watched two hundred movies a year in his stint as a film critic in his early thirties—and the roaming camera gave him a sense of how point of view is always provisional, and always changing, and how we can shadow a character in all his stumblings, so that we feel him bumping around in the dark and don't just watch him from on high. He was also part of the first generation to grow up with the airplane—one title he had proposed for his autobiography was *110 Airports*—and this habit of mobility, touching down in Cuba or Saigon or Tahiti only days after he'd been in England, gave him a sense of how much wider the world is than our minds and how much the truths and certainties of London look like folly when you're sitting in Havana, or vice versa.

Part of his special skill was to learn from the camera how to tell a story out of sequence and with a minimum of distraction—dialogue should be a form of action, he contended, and his slow, often heart-torn sentences are always pushing forwards—even as the real question at the core of every novel is whether the figure at its center will somehow survive, to face more doubts. A complex tale of murder and betrayal is put together like a jigsaw puzzle in *The Quiet American,* with a disappearance at the beginning to cast a shadow over any happiness that follows; but what lingers with us is not the temporary resolution or the economic stitching together of several themes and plots—it's the sense of hauntedness, and irresolution. "Everything had gone right for me," the narrator says in the last sentence of that book, "but how I wished there existed someone to whom I could say that I was sorry."

∴

We waited, my mother and Hiroko and I, for day after long day in our temporary lodging, looking up at the hills in the distance or, in my case, not looking up at all, for fear of what I would see. For night after night I dreamed of fire—three straight nights—and each time, when I awoke, it was with the sense, unanswerable, that our house was gone. I would never see it again, my unconscious seemed to be telling me.

When the earlier fire had burned down our house—and four hundred and twenty-six others—it had come as a sudden, one-night epiphany. A wildfire had broken out on a distant ridge at six in the afternoon; within ten minutes or so it was all around our home. I had fled to a lower spot, trapped for three hours as I watched the outlines of our lives stripped away, and by the end of the night nearly all the damage had been done. The fire, whipped on by "sundowner" winds, roared down from the hills into the crowded residential areas and then

jumped the six lanes of the freeway, seemingly intent on passing through every neighborhood until it reached the sea.

This time there was none of the sudden shock and quick
release into a world of ashes. Day after day we looked up and
saw smoke now surrounding our house, now seeming to have
left, and each day, as the sun set, we girded ourselves for late-
afternoon winds suddenly to pick up and send the flames skit-
tering, unstoppably, in the direction of the town again. The
local newspaper told us that the fire chief himself expected
to lose a hundred houses—ours and all our neighbors'—the
night we evacuated; "the whole bloody world's on fire," as a
fire officer in Greene's Blitz had memorably put it.

In time, after ten days or so, the wind blew the flames up
over the top of the mountain and away from all structures,
and, thanks mostly to the firemen who formed a single line
to stand the blaze down, we and those around us were safe—
until the next time. We drove back to the house; we unpacked
the boxes stuffed with papers and passports and jewelry and
objects of sentimental importance again. Sometimes we were
lucky, it seemed; sometimes we were not. The only lesson the
fire taught was that you never know what will happen next—
our destinies can unravel even as we think we're writing them.

Hiroko and I returned to Japan a few weeks later and summer began to subside, giving way to the peaceful blaze of
autumn. Then, in mid-November, at least a month after "fire
season" ended, I was talking to my mother on the phone when
she said, "I went out with a friend to see a movie last night,
but as soon as we passed the turn, midway down the hill, I saw
huge flames around the town. It looked a long way away, but
you know how it is. The winds were moving at sixty miles per
hour.

"I told Nancy, 'You go to the movie. I'm afraid if I go, I'll just be worrying every moment. Would you mind dropping me home again?'"

That was where she was now, she said, and the fire was, so far, on the other side of town. Before the day was over, though, I heard of a friend who'd lost his house. The brother of another friend went to a movie and came out to be told that he couldn't drive home and, in any case, he had no home to drive to. The fire was moving so quickly that more than two hundred houses were destroyed, many before firefighters had had the chance to react.

The one item that all the media covered—I heard it as soon as it happened, from a newspaper editor in Los Angeles—was that a monastery in the hills, Mount Calvary, the place where Hiroko and I had gone to collect ourselves as our home and my usual monastery up the coast in Big Sur were threatened, was one of the first buildings to go; the sanctuary I'd begun to turn to, with its polished silence and its humbling views over the town and the Pacific, was now nothing but ash.

Six months later, I flew back to Santa Barbara from New York, and arrived at the airport to see a roar of fire rising over a ridge just behind our house and storming down towards it again. This time—Greene's work could have told me this—an "evacuation warning" was issued to the entire town.

CHAPTER 10

I was almost thirty-eight when my sense of Greene was burned to the ground. I knew him inside out by then, I liked to think, in all his many faces: I knew his guardedness, precisely because of all the feelings that were rising inside him; I knew his inability to settle to faith, or to any definition anyone was likely to impose on him; I knew his kindness, the stronger because of the obscure sense of darkness and treachery he always carried with him. When he wasn't fleeing boredom, he was simply trying to escape the familiar—the emotional obligations of making a family—moving from one place to another, one woman to the next as if to tell them, as well as himself, that there was less danger that way of hurting anyone.

He couldn't easily stay with another soul, yet he had a lifelong, almost visceral terror of giving pain (he had always fainted at the mere mention of an accident); he longed to find love, and the peace it might bring, and yet he knew that he would always recoil from commitment, and the prospect it brought of losing everything (or gaining fixity, and obligation);

he spent his whole life searching for a haven that, were he to find it, he would only exile himself from or spoil, and then begin the search again.

Just then, his authorized biographer brought out his second volume of Greene's life, covering the middle years, and I, like many others, read for the first time the letters Greene had written to Catherine Walston, from the time they met through the time when their passion finally began to spark out, more than a dozen years later. The letters were a revelation, volcanic; seldom had I read any appeals, declarations or promises so passionately unguarded and from the heart, it seemed. It was like suddenly seeing a wildfire blaze above the hills, next to which Greene, Catherine, the families they were deserting came to look like silhouettes against a wall of flames.

"I can't get you out of my heart. You've splintered inside it and surgeons are useless. They say one day I may die of the splinter, but it cannot be removed." "How one can go on *falling* in love with the same person . . . sometimes several times a day. My God how I miss you." "I can't get you out of my mind & I don't know how to keep going." "I've never dared to write like this to another person, or wanted to. Dear heart. I am all yours. I can only offer myself to God through you."

Perhaps many a man might write like this at the beginning of an infatuation, the more so if he is an eloquent man, at once relieved to get all his feelings out and a little excited by all that's being released. The words themselves are as reckless and even generic as those of the novelist Greene, measuring out his five hundred words a day, are drily precise and melancholy. Yet on and on they continued, for more than a decade, long after the first disappointments, the first betrayals, the realization of all that would not be possible were far behind the couple.

"Marry me, Catherine . . . How many times one writes the same words till they must be stale as dry bread to you, that never has one conceived the possibility of living so completely before." "No one has ever been more loved than you except the saints." "I'm lost. I don't know what to believe any more. Please pray for me as you've never done before." "You are all I have in the world & I make such a mess of things. Pray for me."

More than once I had to put the letters down; it was like picking up a casserole dish straight from the oven. In a way, they confirmed everything I liked to believe of Greene; by bringing his heart to the surface, they showed precisely the tender, solicitous, generous and fervent man whom otherwise he tried to keep hidden (or, in his books, powerfully imminent). It was like seeing the soul, intimate and beseeching, emerge from behind the personality. He was still as treacherous and inconstant and sometimes bitter to Catherine as he showed himself to be in his novels; it must have been terrifying, I thought, to be on the receiving end of such letters— and Catherine had replied (and perhaps fanned the flames) by keeping him at a distance, suggesting their relationship remain platonic, even telling him of her affairs with other men. Sometimes it could seem as if it was the very fact that she was so difficult to hold that drove him on, even as she was reflecting back to him exactly the burdened sense of duty, the changing faces, the reluctance to stay put that he brought to others.

Yet it was like having a bet paid off, and a friendship vindicated, the way I'd felt when Louis, without a moment's hesitation, had thrown aside his wailing renditions of Sam Cooke's "Chain Gang" to race into the empty road in Ethiopia to tend to two strangers in need.

The classic Englishman—I thought of Maugham again, and

John le Carré—is especially ardent because he's been holding
in his feelings so long, and for Greene this sudden love made
sense only because it was instantaneous, out of control and, in
some ways, senseless (Catherine had four small children and,
as a Catholic, was particularly unlikely to give herself over to
him, which perhaps made him feel both safer and more fired
by the hunt). It came in the face of his habitual doubts, his
forty-two years of failing to find a place for faith, his knowledge of how much he should know better. I thought of the
moment in *The Quiet American* that lies at the heart of the
story when Fowler, so intent on presenting himself as unin-
volved and beyond youthful caring, goes into the toilet of the
American Legation, certain at last that he's lost Phuong, and
collapses into tears of jealousy and pain.

Just then, on something of a whim—perhaps I wanted to
revisit my hometown of Oxford with Greene, and see him
anew in the light of these burning letters—I decided to go
back for the first time to the initial volume of the biography,
which I'd ignored when it came out, not wanting the art to
be obscured by the life. When I did so, I was shocked. Midway through the book, Greene is approached by the young
reader, Vivien, and, very soon, he is pouring out the same kind
of torrent to her, when he is only twenty. Out comes a flood of
charming, boyish, ingenious messages—letters in code, antic
flights, veiled emotional threats, words of adoration that might
be laid before a saint. In two and a half years, according to
the biography, the young Greene sent the virginal Catholic
teenager two thousand letters, often up to three a day, literally counting the moments till they would meet. When he saw
how much Norman Sherry quoted from these letters in his
book, the aging Greene was so upset that he made his bump-

tious Texan Boswell weep; he never seemed to mind if someone revealed his cruelties, his lies, his betrayals—he appeared almost to thrive on that, and the relief of being found out—but if someone made public his tender and adoring heart, he flinched.

"Dear love, dear only love for ever, dear heart's desire. I'm aching for you, I need you as much as any cripple might." "Come back to me & I'll soon make you believe again that I shall love you as long as life & if there's life after, afterwards." "My miracle-worker . . . You've given trees shade, and the flowers scent, and the sun a gold it's never had before." "More than earth / More than fire / More than light / Darling."

He would kneel before God, he wrote to Vivien, if only she would marry him; he would honor her wish for celibacy, if only they could be wed. In truth he did become a Catholic just so she would accept him. Yet, as with Catherine more than twenty years later, he seemed to be courting his love as the true object of his faith; it was less that she would bring him to God than that he would use God as a way to get her heart. "You are my saint," he wrote to Vivien (just as the young boy in his first novel, *The Man Within,* thinks of the girl he meets in his fairy-tale cottage); "miracles will be done at your grave." "You are simply the symbol of the Absolute," he writes. The deeply devout woman who had written him about the Virgin Mary must have been more than a little unsettled by the intensity and wondered why he seemed to be prostrating himself not before God but fallible her.

It was as if there was a question mark where his heart should be, and perhaps he could answer it only with such passion; it was hard, reading Greene, to forget that he had titled one play *Yes and No* and seemed to live in an eternal maybe.

Always impatient with anyone who would put his faith in an abstraction, able only to repose his confidence in the wavering heart, he seemed almost to need to solve the riddle of belief by taking a leap of faith towards another mortal. The passionate letters might have been a way of trying to will himself into conviction and trust, because he knew and feared that, soon, very soon, his foothold would begin to slip and he would be in the abyss again.

A woman came to my apartment once when I was living in New York City, in my mid-twenties, having asked me, and asked me, for five weeks when I would be free (I should have said, "Never," but perhaps I, too, was not yet ready to close the door on possibility). We'd met a couple of months before, and I'd found her to be bright, quick and fun, a recent student of my father's in California who'd made contact with me after she'd read a long piece I'd written for *Time* magazine on the cocaine trade. Kristin (she shared a name with my college girlfriend) was bursting with life and spirit, but I was on my way to Asia for many months and she was living with her college boyfriend, and, through the vagaries that made me like corn, say, but never eggs, I knew she would never be my type.

When I offered her some juice, though, soon after she arrived, she slipped something into my glass ("ADAM," as she would later explain, her fond nickname for the new drug that was just beginning to make itself known in New York, MDMA, or Ecstasy). For thirty minutes or so I felt a wild pounding of the heart (she sat next to me, clearly shaken by what she'd unloosed). Then, very suddenly, I was in love with her, a perfectly attractive person I'd have walked by on the street, a hundred times a day, without noticing.

She stayed with me for the sixteen or eighteen hours the drug's effect was said to last, but after she left, it didn't begin to subside. I started writing letters to her, feverish, long letters that went on for page after page. I went to my office, to write more endless articles on the violent struggle around apartheid in South Africa, the killing of Ninoy Aquino in the Philippines, but really all I was doing was turning from my typewriter to my desk to scribble out page after page of handwritten madness. Kristin didn't know quite what to do with this—whatever hopes she'd had the night had ended—but she gamely took responsibility for the spirit she'd released.

In time, after two and a half months or so, and seventy days of writing five, ten pages a day, the tablet's effect faded, and I never looked at the love drugs of A *Midsummer Night's Dream* with quite the same skepticism again. We ended up, through a small miracle, as fast friends who'd somehow come out on the far side of a romance, intimate and trusting, without ever having had a relationship. But Kristin was not the only one to wonder what in the world had happened. How much does a drug, an infatuation, place feelings inside one, and how much does it only uncover what was there all along? And how true, how deep were all the sentiments that came pouring out of me? Were they aimed at her, at the excitement of covering pages or just, at some level, at the feeling itself, intoxication?

∴

So much of writing is a performance, a design or presentation aimed to charm or divert or persuade; the great challenge of the desk is to push past every agenda and self-consciousness to whatever lies beneath. Greene often said that he could not imagine how anyone could handle the shocks and confusions of a regular life without the catharsis and the clarifying agent of a pen. And the reason I loved him and he moved me so much was that he had the gift of seeming at last to set aside his evasions and false selves as soon as he began writing in another voice (in nonfiction, he could be as hard to catch as he no doubt was in life).

But what came out of his honest self-reckonings were always new questions about himself. Jim, the young protagonist of his last published novel, comes, after many years, upon the letters of the slippery character who's taken him under his wing and is always leaving behind the woman he loves, and he is shamed, silenced by their obvious sincerity, their almost painful solicitude. By contrast, Jim reflects, as he sits in his "two-roomed flat," trying to become a writer, he completes rough drafts even for his love letters, and in his most private correspondence "worked hard to produce the maximum effect on the reader." At the end of his life, Greene seems to be wondering, through his final alter ego, if he's ever loved at all—the same question that has haunted all his novels, full of feeling and sympathy and pathos as they are.

Sometimes I'd wondered the same thing about my father, or even myself; words came so easily to him that I could not tell how much he was inside them, how much outside, knowing just the effect that eloquence can have. Or maybe, I often thought, he himself could not tell how true or how deep his sentences were—as he spoke with such unstoppable fluency on silence and the need to leave all words behind—and from which place inside him they came. I'd turned to writing because it offered few escape routes or hiding places; it's harder to lie to yourself on the page than in the world. But of course living with words had moved me to trust most those moments that come only when words run out.

On first meeting the letters to Catherine, I'd liked to believe that she had freed Greene at last from second thoughts, offering him passion without a real threat of domesticity; he'd asked her again and again to marry him, but he surely knew that he could no more easily settle to her, ultimately, than to himself. If he got his wish, he'd soon long to undo it. But to find him making the same protests of eternal devotion half a lifetime before, to a woman who could not have been more different (part of Catherine's appeal was surely that she was Vivien's wild opposite) was like having his most naked confessions in church doubted.

The only consolation—though was it one?—was that Greene, as always, seemed to be wise to his own maneuvers. In *The Quiet American,* his middle-aged Englishman writes to the wife he's abandoned back in England to ask for a divorce (exactly the kind of scene I could imagine being incited in life by Greene's sudden passion for Catherine). She responds to him, in what sounds like his own wife's voice, full of the same undeluded calm and clarity: "You say it will be the end of life to lose this girl. Once you used exactly that phrase to me—I could show you the letter, I have it still—and I suppose you wrote in the same way to Anne. You say that we've always tried to tell the truth to each other, but, Thomas, your truth is always so temporary."

∴

The questions tore at me because all Greene's books are, deep down, about the shaking of the heart, and not the body. It's easier to find concrete evidence for sex than for love, so his official biographer, Norman Sherry, eagerly visited a brothel in Haiti to cross-question a madam on her long-ago client, and his dark counter, the American critic Michael Shelden, who all but accuses Greene of murder, recorded the testimony of a chambermaid in Jamaica as to the state of Greene's sheets after he had been staying there with Catherine. But always I remembered Fowler, in *The Quiet American,* in one of his moments of sudden candor, saying, "None of us needs it as much as we say." He's had only four loves in his life, he says, and he wonders what the other forty or so partners were all about.

No one talks about sex so much as a schoolboy who knows next to nothing about it, and sometimes I wondered if Greene, like many of his protagonists, was only pretending to be wicked; he made such a big display of his interest in sex shows and brothels that it was easy to believe, as his friend Malcolm Muggeridge said, that he was a "sinner manqué." A friend of mine sent Greene a novel he'd written, and the only word the older novelist objected to in it was "panties" ("Couldn't you use 'step-ins'?" was his bizarre suggestion.) It's remarkable how, a decade after Lady Chatterley, Greene chose never to go much into sex at all in his books, even as he was offering to risk imprisonment to bring *Lolita* into print in England.

His women were friends at least as much as they were loves; he stayed in close contact with Dorothy and Catherine and Anita Björk until death intervened, and his need for intimacy (call it absolution or just understanding) seemed at least as strong as his need for apartness. He came to life around women, every one of his friends told me; but clearly, too, women came to life around him. They could feel his vulnerability, which he never tried to hide, his strange mixture of shyness and need, and they could see that he put feelings before everything (in his books at least) and kindness before mere doctrine. Sometimes I suspected that he really did believe, with a curious innocence, that it made sense to turn to professional lovers because there was no chance of betraying them; tenderness would come without a price tag (or, more precisely, with a financial price tag, which would always be easier to take care of).

∴

In Toronto, one hot summer at the beginning of the new century, I happened to be one of fifty-eight people asked to talk for twenty minutes, onstage in a large theater, on our passion of the moment (I, too typically, spoke about the new possibilities of our global order, and the way it allowed for multiple homes and multiple selves). One evening, one of the only other writers there sought me out and started to talk about the writers she especially loved.

"What about you?" she asked.

"Well, I've been preoccupied for many years with Graham Greene."

Her face lit up. "That story of his," she said. "You know 'The Blue Film'?"

"The one about the man in Bangkok who takes his wife to see a 'French film' in a little hut? And then realizes that the man undressing in the movie is himself, thirty years before? With the only woman he's ever truly loved, a street girl hired for the picture?"

"Right," she said. "Every time I read it, I cry."

It looked to me as if she was close to tears now; she seemed to waver a little in the glossy atrium of the high-tech building where we were being served canapés. She had, as it turned out, been a professional call girl herself—that was what she wrote about—and now maintained a column on the intricacies of male-female relations, as seen from her unusual perspective. Perhaps she knew, I thought, about those men who wanted to be held as much as touched; perhaps someone like her could read a man like Greene in the dark.

CHAPTER 11

One day, almost by mistake, I stumbled upon a perfect description of Graham Greene—coming, curiously enough, from a daughter. "He never seems to like a steady diet of any one thing or person," she had said, and "has an overwhelming horror of being bored." Since he also had an "overpowering hatred of hurting people," this meant that he was often in flight from society, afraid of being oppressed, and fell into what his biographer called an "extraordinary restlessness" as he tried to outrun the "deep, inner wound of his childhood."

The only problem was that the person being described there was not Graham Greene, but P. G. Wodehouse.

Not much later, I came across the following: "His eyes were an intense blue. I thought that here was a man who had seen a lot of the world, who was experienced, and yet who seemed to have suffered . . . He had a gift for creating an atmosphere of such intimacy that I found myself talking freely to him. I was impressed by his beautiful manners."

Yet the woman who delivered this, Eleanor Brewer, was

here talking, again, not of Greene, but of his famously traitorous friend and sometime colleague, Kim Philby, who had once said, after defecting to Moscow, that all he wanted in life was "Graham Greene on the other side of the table, and a bottle of wine between us." Brewer was not completely unworldly; she was married to the chief Middle Eastern correspondent for *The New York Times* in Beirut at the time she fell under Philby's spell and left her husband to become his third wife. But he'd gotten under her skin with the notes he'd written, sometimes several every day.

"Deeper in love than ever, my darling," he wrote to Brewer, on pieces of paper taken from cigarette packs. "Deeper and deeper, my darling."

∴

So there I was again: the man I felt such closeness to was a type, and there were many others of his background who matched aspects of his type to the letter. Yet it was only Greene I saw when I looked into the mirror of what I'd written, and only his unholy book I found next to the Gideons' Bible in a foreign hotel room, as if slipped there by some intruder. It liked to say, his gospel for the fallen, that all of us know what we're supposed to do—trust in God, trust in ourselves, remember that "this too shall pass"—but that none of that helps us when we're looking for consolation in the dark. It said that wisdom is wonderful on a mountaintop, but that in the world an unwise man might have more to offer us than any sage does. It said that what we don't know is more likely to save us than what we do know.

The fugitive priest at the center of *The Power and the Glory,* a moth-eaten, unshaven man with the air of "somebody of no account who had been beaten up" is described, early on, as a "black question mark, ready to go, ready to stay, poised on his chair": the archetypal Greene protagonist. But only twenty pages later, the ruthless lieutenant who is pursuing him is similarly described: "a little dark menacing question-mark in the sun." The Captain, in Greene's final novel, more than sixty years on, is "an eternal questionmark never to be answered, like the existence of God." When Greene, one New Year's night in Stockholm, picked out a fortune from a pool, it turned out to be a question mark. All his novels are unreliable gospels for those who can't be sure of a thing.

∴

I was in Bogotá one grey day in July—the city Greene once sailed towards, with Henry James, in a dream—and church bells were ringing around the deserted business area in the north of the city where I was staying. As ever, the hills that encircle the place, thickly forested, were swathed in clouds, and it looked about to rain, about not to rain, at any moment. A long line of people from the poor parts of town and the countryside snaked around the base of Monserrate, waiting for a cable car to carry them up to the little church at the top of the mountain, above the clouds.

I decided to go out to the city's suburbs with the young volunteer, Maria Paula, who had been deputed by a magazine editor to show me around her town. We traveled away from the broad boulevards and the green-glass skyscrapers of the modern, hopeful area into a disorderly shambles, so rough that Maria Paula put a finger to her lips to remind me not to speak English and draw attention to my foreignness. We walked for ten minutes or more through a marketplace, much of Bogotá surging up the chill steep slopes on the midsummer Sunday morning, till we came to a little plaza where stood a modest red-brick building, and what looked to be a huge hotel beside it.

Inside, it was so crowded we could hardly move. People were pushing and crushing and being pushed into a little shrine where sat a Holy Infant, the protective treasure of the Iglesia 20 de Julio. Some were dressed in the heavy woolen ponchos of the interior and had wrinkled, pre-Colombian features; others were Indian women in bowler hats, as from the Andes; the young blades of Bogotá were here, with their gangsta ways and their girls, and lanky black guys, from the Caribbean coast, towering above the crowd. Colombia was more crisscrossed with factions and almost unimaginable brutality than any country in the Americas: the leftist guerrillas were fighting the government soldiers and groups of paramilitary vigilantes were trying to get the better of the guerrillas by cutting off tongues and quartering victims with chainsaws; the *narcotraficantes* had been responsible for cities like Medellín boasting the highest murder rate in the world; and two days after I visited the church, a daring government rescue mission would retrieve the former presidential candidate, Íngrid Betancourt, who had been held by guerrilla kidnappers, along with fourteen others, for more than six years.

But now, as far as I could see—and Maria Paula agreed—all the feuding groups were here, in the crowds swelling the aisles of the main church, clapping along as an acoustic guitar was strummed softly, far away at the front, unseeably far, while a lone female voice struck up the sweet chorus.

"¡No pasarán!" said Maria Paula, speaking to me, but also joining in the refrain—a folk song that could have been serving as an international anthem—and when the priest spoke again, mothers held up babies, worn campesinos held up bottles, or copies of the day's schedule, to try to receive blessings from the altar at the front.

I walked around amidst the faces of the country, not wanting to romanticize this tough and often menacing place, or see what wasn't there; if I found innocence here, it was only because I couldn't read the signs, or didn't know what to look for. Young girls were snuggling up against their novios, who looked very much as if they were about to go to war (for the leftists or their enemies, I couldn't tell). Beggars in their forties, with thin, uncared-for hair, put up their palms for blessings, closed their eyes to the strummed guitar. Families kept shuffling in and out of the interior—a perpetual commotion—as clapping rose from the overflow crowd next door.

"You won't find this in the rich areas," said Maria Paula, who belonged so staunchly to those areas that she had been worried about stepping outside them today, except that she remembered coming to the church with her grandmother. "The power of hope is great."

"Prepaid" women, as she engagingly translated the term, stood by their mafiosi protectors, and hit men and soldiers and fighters who had lost limbs to the mafiosi joined in the song. The man next to me had a bleached spot on his cheek; others had scars all across their faces. Nobody looked very safe or happy for long.

I remembered the one previous time I'd come to the city, at

eighteen, with my friend from high school. We'd ended up in a completely unlit area—Colombians shivered as I described the scene for them now—where girls in hot pants and men with guns roamed up and down the barely paved lanes. Like innocents from Greene's *Monsignor Quixote* (we anticipated the scene from that novel by just seven years), we were the only residents of the Hotel Picasso who never thought to wonder why all the other guests of the hotel were young, female and very scantily clad, much more ready to say hello to us than anyone else we'd met on our trip so far had been.

Maria Paula and I spent a long time in the church—it was the first time I'd felt at all close to the heart of Colombia—and then we walked (a finger to the lip again) back through the sloping streets where families were gathering in broken little cantinas for Sunday lunch and into the chaos of the marketplace, to find a taxi driver who would not grow too hungry or suspicious if we asked him to take us to the rich side of town.

"I wasn't expecting much of this," I said that night at a Mexican restaurant, talking with the only other writer from the United States who had defied a State Department warning to come here to speak on the state of the world. "Today, onstage, a woman started talking to me about V. S. Naipaul's wounds and asked me what mine were."

"What did you say?"

"Something about detachment. Not being good at settling down."

"What about Greene? What do you think his wound was?"

I said nothing for a moment, untypically. "Doubt," I came out with at last. "The fact that he could never give himself entirely to a person or a faith, even though his conscience was alive enough to know that not to do so was untenable."

We fell silent then, and my mind went back to the little children, the dirty ponchos, the clapping that had greeted the end of the service that morning. Hoodlums coming in and out, bearing babies on their shoulders, drug dealers cupping their girls tenderly at the small of their backs, soldiers taking off their caps and then leading their grandmothers towards the Holy Infant.

∴

It was the oddest thing, I thought as I walked around the streets of Bogotá the next day, not knowing who was who and what to make of them, but what Greene had really done, for me at least, was dismantle the entire notion of an "enemy." Holy books, again, teach us about kindness and forgiveness and union; he, much too typically, taught us, as he liked to put it, about "hate." We know, more or less, what to do with our friends; it's our seeming enemies who pose problems—and therefore possibilities—at the core.

The adulterer Bendrix, in Greene's most passionate novel, *The End of the Affair*, ends up not just moving in with the husband he's cuckolded, but going on long walks with him, his hand protectively on his rival's arm; they begin to seem like a couple brought together by the great love they have in common. Wormold, the shy lost father in Havana, finds himself at the climax of his story playing checkers with a notorious Cuban police officer who is said to carry a cigarette case made of human skin. But he learns, as the night goes on, that the case is not a sadist's relic of some innocent the man has tortured; it's a reminder of what was done to his father. All

Segura is doing, in effect, is carrying his father's skin round with him.

In *The Quiet American,* the unquiet Englishman makes it a defining principle to dislike and deride the quiet American, and the quiet American appoints himself Fowler's rival in love as well as politics. Yet much of the anguish and complication of the book, its bitter intensity, comes from the fact that each has only the other to confide in in a very foreign country, and neither knows what to do with the affection and sense of solicitude they feel developing between them. *The Quiet American* is much more about the difficult, treacherous love between the two male rivals than about the love either feels for Phuong.

The great religious books and teachers tell us to love our neighbor as ourself, to do unto others as you would have them do unto you, to put white before black. But Greene asks what happens if the neighbor you're loving is, in fact, your neighbor's wife. He asks why you would ever do to someone what you want him to do to you—because what you feel you deserve at his hands is retribution. He tells us that black and white are figments of the imagination; the deeper you see anything, the less you can reach for absolutes. "Sometimes we have a kind of love for our enemies," as Fowler says, in a political context, "and sometimes we feel hate for our friends." It can sound like a pretty, too-Greenian paradox until you realize that in his books, as in many lives, enemies do suddenly become friends and then turn enemy again.

Whenever I read Greene—he mocks America's civilization, yet his greatest love was an American, as was his favorite writer; he constantly pricks holes in Catholicism, yet his fallen, errant, sinning Catholic priest becomes a hero precisely because he refuses to flee when a dying mother needs his priestly ministration—I noticed that the only reliable and constant enemy in all his work was, in fact, a version of himself. That was the way in which he was most deeply Catholic, if only in a backwards way: that he never gave himself the benefit of the doubt and always assumed that the other man had a point. And whatever woes his protagonists face, the challenges never seem quite arbitrary, and they have to assume that they've done something to deserve them. The fact we can't argue with our own fate is what renders us bereft.

"Inexorably the other's point of view rose on the path like a murdered innocence," he wrote, in *The Heart of the Matter,* and the very violence of the phrasing shows how alive and terrible the pain was. "Hate was just a failure of imagination," he wrote in *The Power and the Glory,* more or less compressing his belief and reason for writing into seven simple words. All Greene's work is about the conundrum of feeling someone else's position too acutely, to the point of not being able to hear, or act on, one's own. And that natural sympathy for the other's point of view is made more agonized—more complex—because one can have so little faith in oneself. Greene could write with harrowing compassion for every character except the one who might be taken as Graham Greene.

When his old boss and drinking buddy Kim Philby defected to the Soviet Union, having sent many innocent Englishmen to their deaths, Greene horrified many by remaining loyal to him, going three times in a year to visit him in Moscow and even writing the foreword to Philby's memoir about his treacheries. Greene's biographer Norman Sherry writes that he never felt "the pale compelling hardness" of Greene's eyes, enraged, so much as when he, Sherry, dared (as most people did) to question Philby's integrity. For Greene, Philby had a dedication to his cause (however mistaken) that the novelist envied and that put him to shame; and for Greene, loyalty to a friend was always as impossible to doubt as devotion to an abstraction was impossible to believe. "Would the world be in the mess it is," asks Wormold in *Our Man in Havana* (and it is a refrain that runs through much of Greene), "if we were loyal to love and not to countries?"

And when Sherry spent a long day with Greene, and the issue of the novelist's enemies came up, Greene went away, consulted his brother Hugh and, a little later, volunteered a list of all the people who might have something to say against him. It was characteristic of a man who seemed to have no interest in self-exoneration and was ready to convict himself of virtually every sin. Greene could not bring himself to believe in God and so, by his own lights, he was cursed. But he could not entirely believe in himself or his own positions, including his arguments against God, and so there was always a small chink of hope.

Fathers

CHAPTER 12

A fter I left the Dragon School, at the age of thirteen, I and many of my classmates found ourselves in an even older all-male institution, somewhere between the grey towns of Slough and Windsor, interned within New Buildings (so called because they contained the oldest classroom in the world, from 1440). Our little studies—every boy had a room of his own—looked out on a cobbled courtyard, a clock tower and a statue of our distant patron, Henry VI; the fields around us were called Agar's Plough, Sixpenny and—too perfectly—Mesopotamia. Every morning, at 6:45, a white-coated retainer of sorts, Mr. Gower, knocked on each door, and opened it a crack—"Morn, sir!"—and then we trudged down the icy stone spiral staircase to where a vat of tea and our copies of *The Times* awaited us.

The fields were still wet with dew as we walked across them to the first class of the morning—Caesar most likely—at 7:30. Then we wandered back across the grass to kippers or porridge in our old wooden hall and, putting on white surplices over the full morning dress (black tails and white ties) we had to wear each day, with black gowns on top, marched in a solemn line, singing, "Immortal, Invisible, God only wise," to our places in the near-cathedral across the courtyard. Bells tolled to summon us to prayer, across the cloisters where sat our copy of the Gutenberg Bible, through the long passageways with names of the departed along the walls, into the little rooms where, as the Dame's patrolling feet were heard each night at 9:00, we buried ourselves with copies of Richard Brautigan, Hunter Thompson, the sea-mail copy of *The Village Voice* that found me every week, two months late.

When we had to recite passages from the classics—I mischievously chose *Siddhartha* for my text, smuggling a piece of California into rainy Berkshire—we stood among busts of Wellington and Gladstone and my father's hero Shelley; their names were inscribed in the walls and desks all round, to remind us of where duty beckoned. In the drizzly afternoons of October we ran a "Steeplechase," as horses might, for five miles across the mud, splashing near the end across a fifteen-foot stream, and as the cold and damp grew ever deeper, we assembled by the Wall in late November for a game played nowhere else in the world. One boy sat on a ball, nineteen larger boys, from two teams, sat on top of him, everyone was invited to punch and pummel everyone else (though the rules specifically forbade "gouging out an eye") and no one, by tradition, mentioned that the last goal scored had come in 1909.

I didn't resent all this, however much I was sometimes unnerved by it; as the years went on, I came to think that this was the kind of system, refined and perfected over centuries, that knew exactly how to cherish and encourage freedom precisely by placing it within clear limits. The school had acres and acres of grounds—rivers running along under stone bridges, secret gardens tucked among the elms, a whole town that had grown up round it—and on several afternoons a week we had all our hours free after lunch (though two or three essays to write by the next morning). We were being trained, in effect, to rule ourselves and to become masters of time; as president of the Chess Club, I used the special key I was given to admit myself into a private library, lavish with sofas, eighteenth-century portraits above the fireplaces, shelves and shelves of books in several rooms, and no one to disturb the peace for hours.

I could write my essays—"Antony is just an aging rake: discuss" "Offer a five-year economic plan for the newly independent nation of Malawi" (easily done if, as I did, you contacted the Malawian embassy in London and requested its assistance for ideas)—and then still come out by late afternoon to play games of tennis next to the King of Siam's Garden or gather in the drinking place to which every boy had access as soon as he turned sixteen.

At the end of each term, and "Trials," as they were called, all 250 boys in the year assembled in a large auditorium so that everyone could be told precisely who had placed 1st, and who 51st, and who 249th and 250th. Privileges for years thereafter—could we have a record player in our rooms, were we allowed into the in-house library?—depended on these standings. As younger boys, we had to be servants of the elders, shining their shoes every day, bringing them their newspaper in the morning, starting their fires in the winter; every time the deafening call "Boy Upppp!" rang through the corridors, we had to drop everything we were doing (homework, most likely) and hurtle up to the source of the cry. The last one there had to race across town to fetch an older boy a magazine, or deliver a message for him. Older boys were allowed to beat younger (as masters were not), and rumors gleefully recalled that, if bored, our seniors would summon a few juniors, ask them to spread out their hands on a table and, blindfolded, jab among the fingers with their compasses.

Bad pieces of work were torn in two in front of the whole class, and we were ranked in every single subject every two weeks, obliged to take our report cards to be inspected by two separate overseers; yet one beauty of the system—even we could see—was that we were in the hands of men, often Old Boys themselves, who had one great skill in life, and that was the management of hormone-addled, restless, adolescent boys. Our parents became liberators, the bringers of possibility we were delighted to see, and all the struggles of puberty played out in other lives at home, leaving scars and sometimes enmities for life, were here handled by impersonal agents of authority, whom we had no qualms about leaving behind or defying, even as our parents (or mine at least) spoiled us with condolences and trips to the movies and freedom to stay up past nine o'clock.

Each time I flew back, in fact, to visit my mother and father, it was like stepping out of a formal, intimate dance, a costume drama in a garden maze, and into absolute emptiness again. Just as when we'd first moved to California several years before. None of the words I learned in our ancient classrooms carried, and nothing in post-'60s California made much sense within our grey-stone cloisters. It was like flying between different dimensions of the mind, and one world could no more understand the other than I, in a skeptical mood, could feel sudden moments of rapturous transport, or, when dreaming, could begin to make out the parade-ground rat-a-tat-tat of reason.

At school, when we were allowed to put on a play without any help from teachers, we chose, almost inevitably, the fiendishly complex and malevolent Jacobean drama *The Revenger's Tragedy*, and I found myself playing an illegitimate prince who has slaughtered his father and is now lasciviously wooing his mother (a part taken on for us by a master's daughter with the highly typical name of Iona Stormonth Darling). No one could much appreciate this in Santa Barbara, even though I pointed them towards the cool new Pynchon novel that reenacted a Jacobean drama within suburban, acid-dropping Southern California.

When I flew back to England, after three or four weeks of license, it was into a world where most of us decorated our rooms with black-light posters and secretly slipped one another copies of *Ladies of the Canyon*, at least one in our class along the paths around Hardy's Wessex clearly tripping in some deeper way. Saturnalia and the Revolution were irresistible here only because they were so far away, and existed mostly in our heads. It was like moving through some allegory between a City of Hope, where history has been abolished, and a City of History, where hope can be slipped in only as contraband, a highly illicit substance.

I was moving, I suppose, every three months, between the worlds of Fowler and Pyle. *The Quiet American* could never be just a book to me; it was like a diagram of the world I knew, my boyhood, and every time I picked it up, it was like being on the plane again, moving in either direction, between young Americans who were engagingly full of ideas of salvation and self-improvement and Brits who reflexively claimed to believe in nothing at all. It wasn't just that my father was giving his students the classical roots of possibility while we, singing "Holy, Holy, Holy, Lord God Almighty," were receiving a crash

course in reality; it wasn't even just that each of these mutu-
ally incomprehending worlds, almost inevitably, longed for the
other, the Californian kids I knew seeming to yearn for tradition, constancy, even (though it was rarely stated) hierarchy,
while my English friends, when they came to visit, instantly
asked if we could drive up to Esalen.

It was something deeper: "What is cowardice in the young
is wisdom in the old," as Greene writes in a late book of stories. "But all the same one can be ashamed of wisdom." That
was the most poignant of all the paradoxes he lived among, as
every one of his characters sought to learn hard truths about
the world and himself, and to come to a place beyond illusion;
and then, once there, wished, at some level, he could be a
young fool again.

If you delivered the title of that book of stories, *May We
Borrow Your Husband?*, in an American voice, it sounded
boyish, polite, full of openness; if you said it in an English
voice, it sounded feline, jaded, even decadent. In the distance
between the two lies the heartbreak.

∴

Greene made it his practice, as I'd admired, never to let
himself off the hook for anything; when people sought
him out for counsel or confession—often priests, convinced
he was the saint of sinners, the only one who understood their
doubts—he invariably told them how hopeless he was and how
different from the person they thought they knew, a cry that
grew more anxious after he appeared on the cover of *Time* in
1951. He sounded, at times, like the convict protagonist in his
friend Narayan's novel, *The Guide*, who is taken to be a sage

the more he protests his unworthiness, and who is acclaimed for his humility even as he simply tells the truth about his many crimes.

Yet deeper than that, I always saw in Greene the boy who sat next to me in class, or who took off on a "Long Run" (he relished such exercises, friends of his told me, because they allowed him to be alone), who clearly had learned well the lesson we were repeatedly taught at school (which left us especially at sea in unembarrassed, aspiring America): that the one thing we should never talk about was our acts of kindness, or selflessness, and what we should always stress were our failures, our faults, and our follies. This was an act of prudence, in part; each of us, after all, was surrounded by 1,249 boys just waiting to sniff out a trace of traitorous goodness. But it was also the principle of the perhaps outdated gentleman's code in which we were being trained: it was unseemly to push yourself forward, or to think very much of yourself at all. When Greene wrote, in *The End of the Affair,* "Virtue tempted him in the dark like a sin"—in *The Power and the Glory,* an errant priest feels "the wild attraction of doing one's duty"—he wasn't just indulging his weakness for paradox; he knew that a certain set of behaviors had been deeply instilled in his characters, and it required courage, the quality he admired most, to stray from them.

We learned this and we learned this, and then I got off TWA 761, in Los Angeles, and found that everything was turned on its head there. People were ashamed of their vices in innocent California, more than of their virtues, and conscience was something to be shouted out, not quietly observed in private; reticence was translated as "repression" and stoicism became "denial." It was as if everything we'd been trained to do and be in England condemned us as corrupt here, and unpardonably complex. Greene noted in *The Quiet American* how "honour" lost a "u" when it went across the Atlantic, but the deeper stress—incurable—was that in the New World "honor" was associated with letting it all hang out, where we had been taught that it lay in keeping things in.

None of this would have mattered much except that I wondered how people in this fresh open society could begin to understand a man who might be keeping quiet about the more sacred or heartfelt parts of his life. And how they could possibly register feeling that was strong precisely because it was not being voiced. How could they ever understand a cry like that of the writer, in *Monsignor Quixote*, "O God, make me human, let me feel temptation. Save me from my indifference"?

Indifference here had been thrown out along with British tea.

∴

A journalist called Ronald Matthews once completed a work with the highly presuming title, *Mon Ami Graham Greene.* Greene, expectably, fought with cold tenacity to ensure that it would never come out in England (it appeared only in France). But, having done so, he also, for no apparent reason, sent Matthews's son through expensive private school and then paid his way through Oxford, and even a year the boy took off. A skeptic might see the outlines of some blackmailing scheme in the charity, but extravagant generosity and a refusal to let himself get away with anything were never out of character in Greene.

He bought his Swedish mistress a house (in part, perhaps, because he could not give her a home), and he bought

another house for the daughter of his French mistress, whom
he spent years defending against the French mafia in his old
age. He bought his French agent a car. He bought a house for
his English mistress Dorothy Glover. He donated thousands
of pounds to the Society of Authors, to help writers less fortunate than he, and, two weeks before his death, with characteristic punctiliousness, he wrote to resign from the same
organization, because he felt he no longer deserved the name
of "author." It took one kind of gift to respond to an Indian
at Oxford who asked him to read a manuscript by an unpub-
lished young friend in faraway India; it took another to spend
the next fifty-six years, until his death, carefully correcting the
English in R. K. Narayan's manuscripts, offering forewords to
his books, serving as his unpaid agent and providing counsel
from afar to a man he didn't meet for twenty years.

"He was a father confessor to me," my old colleague Ber-
nie Diederich told me one thundery night in Coral Gables,
of the man who had been his traveling companion for more
than thirty years, across Central America and in Haiti. "He
always kept his word. Never forgot things. He was very, very
loyal." His "haunted disciple" (in the fine words of the critic
Harold Bloom), John le Carré, singled out Greene's "tran-
scendent universal compassion," as if to identify the one quality he had failed to acquire himself, as a literary heir, for all
the brilliance of his extended portraits of torn loyalties and
the modern search for faith. At times, in fact, it was Greene's
very softheartedness and flinching from brutality (even the
would-be tough Fowler "cannot bear to see another man in
pain") that kept him ever further from belief. "They are always
saying God loves us," a "sort of mother" declares in his final
novel. "If that's love I'd rather have a bit of kindness."

Yet as I went back and forth, in my life and then my head,

between unquiet Englishmen who were often more compassionate than they let on and quiet Americans who were not quite so innocent as they liked to seem, I came to see how much it was a story, in the end, of fathers and sons. The shining children of affluence I knew in California had been told to do their own thing and never to trust anyone over thirty; yet they knew they needed guidance of some kind, and for that they now turned to their elders or the traditions of the East. Louis, meanwhile, was busy devouring James Ellroy's stories of Californian murder and horror as we sat in Haiti—*My Dark Places*—and crooning "Friend of the Devil" to Ethiopian drivers, precisely because he'd never be very far from his inheritance wherever he went. Well into his fifties, like many of my English friends, he was spending weekends, delightedly, with his parents.

Reading *The Quiet American* was like opening the door to some debate inside me that my boyhood had made ceaseless. It was the story of an internal discussion, anguished and unending, between the chivalrous youth in us and the part of us that takes pride in being grown-up and beyond the reach of illusion. Greene was such a master of his craft that, on beginning *A Burnt-Out Case*, for example, he estimated that it would be 65,000 words long (220 pages, in a typical typeface); when he concluded, much, much later, it would come to 64,875 (or 219 and a half pages). To many that would make him too efficient, too settled in his unsettledness; for all the convulsions that made the stories shudder, he knew where they were going and had everything under control. But in *The Quiet American* there is one huge technical flaw that hit me (as many another reader) every time I returned to it. "Like a sandwich?" the young American says. "They're really awfully good." "Oh, I'm so sorry," he says at another point. "It's going to be quite chilly."

Greene was never a master of voices, so perhaps it's no surprise that he couldn't write American. But the deeper truth is that Pyle is just the young quixote and gallant that Fowler had been once upon a time; that in fact is precisely why Fowler so fears him and wants to emphasize his distance from him. The two are more or less the same person, at different stages of life—father and son, you could say, who don't know how much to love each other and how much to compete.

Fowler longs to be disdainful of the young American and retreats into schoolboy mockery every time he's confronted by his good intentions; but that is only, he's almost wise enough to see, because he knows that he wishes those intentions were still his. Over and over he acknowledges that Pyle is in fact a better man for Phuong; his sense of rivalry is persistently haunted by a strange tenderness and almost stealthy solicitude. "I'm glad it's you, Pyle," he says, when the younger man finally takes Phuong away from him (and earlier, he even goes so far as to woo Phuong on Pyle's behalf, because the young American's French isn't up to it). When he visits the quiet American's flat after his death, Fowler pockets for himself as a sentimental keepsake the very book by York Harding, a fictional New World pundit, that he's been deriding throughout the novel.

"I know you better than you do yourself," Pyle at one point says to Fowler. And Fowler's most haunting sentence in the book may well be, "Am I the only one who really cared for Pyle?"

∴

Greene's great theme was always innocence, if only because he could never disguise how much he missed it; most of his stories are set just outside the Gates of Eden, with one character looking back at the hopefulness he's just lost and another, still unfallen, whose imminent exile we ache for. That was part of what always held me in the novels: that none of the characters was entirely cynical, able to write off all belief, and yet none of them can be a simple believer, either. They're all trembling in the balance, and the innocent American who so longs to rescue people kills civilians in the service of his dreams; the Englishman who is so strangely tender and protective towards the young American, as a father might be, plays a part in bringing about his death. The woman they both crave for her sweetness shows a bracing matter-of-factness about her emotions, silently carrying her hopes back and forth between the Grand Canyon and the Cheddar Gorge.

"It's all you write about," the most discerning reader among my friends had said when I was in my twenties: "innocence and its loss." And perhaps the way that both are always inside us as we travel between a father's world and a boy's.

But there was something deeper going on than just the passage between wide-openness and discrimination as I flew back and forth across the Atlantic, from the teachers we called "Twiggy" and "Yakker" and "B.O."—we officially knew them and sometimes ourselves only by their initials—to the Harvard philosophers around our home in Santa Barbara who were so eagerly setting about remaking the world and eliminating humiliation and inequality and struggle (perhaps reality itself) by remaking themselves.

When I thought of my father, I always saw bright colors: the yellow shirts he wore, the house he'd painted the saffron of a Buddhist monk's robes, the mustard-yellow Alfa-Romeo he drove fast around our mountain curves ("Slow down, Ragha-van!" my mother would cry, and he'd accelerate). Some of the time he sat, endearingly rapt, before *South Pacific* on the television, his copies of books on Einstein and Adler piled in high towers around the foot of his blue chair, orange and black folders laid out around them, in a system known only to himself. But always there was a sense of conviction in him, and the bright colors of someone who seemed to know exactly what he thought and wanted others to believe the same.

The Greene I carried in my head was drab-colored and loved to be invisible. Since his earliest years, his mother used to say, he'd hated having attention drawn to him. He longed to disappear into the larger world, I always felt, and he liked to think that shared doubt drew men together more than common faith did. The people he most distrusted in his books were the ones who seemed most sure of themselves.

We run and run from who we are—this was Greene's theme from the beginning—only to discover, of course, that that is precisely what we can never put behind us.

CHAPTER 13

"I loved Greene's sadness," the older American novelist said, as Czechs in high heels and men in suits walked down the imposing steps behind us. We were sitting in the courtyard of the Royal Academy of Arts in Piccadilly, on a blustery summer's day, one of the four days of sunshine permitted every year in Britain by royal decree.

"My mother had trouble with her moods," he went on, "and I was prone to bouts of sadness, too. That was part of what drew me to him. When I was growing up, I never felt I could be Faulkner or Melville or Proust, any of the writers I admired. But I felt I could become Greene. Even though I couldn't, of course." He "had the gift of getting readers to fall in love with him, on the page," another friend who'd known the novelist well, and liked him, told me. "It's what he did. Robert De Niro plays mobsters and he played this part that was hard to resist."

It was never easy for me to come back to England; it was associated with the past, and with a place I knew too well. I knew its limits, I felt, and had exhausted the small range of what was possible there. In Greenian terms, that was proof that this was "home." But I was on an excursion to Turkey at the time, and Mike had gotten in touch, and, without intending it, we'd found ourselves in the heart of Greeneland in its deepest sense: on one side of the main street were the gentlemen's clubs and private tailors that might have spoken for his background, along with the Ritz, where he stayed when he came back to London; on the other was Shepherd Market, which still smelled of perfume and two centuries or more of streetwalkers' incitations.

Mike had gotten to know Greene when he was a young man; a priest had told him to send the older novelist a letter and introduce himself, since he was nearby. He hadn't expected Greene to respond, let alone to be so open and loquacious; though famous, and already living quietly in his "two-roomed" flat in Antibes, Greene had invited him to dinner and soon began talking about sex clubs and his infidelities. "He didn't want to be alone," as Mike saw it. "But he didn't want the burden of obligation, as it were. He never wanted to be part of a coterie, to take in the literary scene."

"That's part of what makes him so alluring. Even approachable. That he always seems to be alone. Weakness is what he wrote from. It was what he wrote about, as well."

"Yes," said Mike, who had also gotten to know many of the other roaming novelists of the time, from Anthony Burgess to Paul Bowles. "There was something defenseless about him. Like a turtle without a shell. He couldn't drive; he had an air of helplessness about him. I think that was part of his appeal to women. The fact he seemed to need taking care of.

"I don't think he did, really, but he gave that impression. When I heard he'd been in Malaya chasing guerrillas, or in the Gaza Strip, a part of me found it hard to believe. He wasn't a very practical man."

I thought of his unfortunate biographer, Norman Sherry,

who had dreamed, I guessed, of becoming the fearless adventurer he took Greene to be. He'd tramped across Liberia, because Greene had done so; he'd contracted dysentery in the same remote mountain village in Mexico—even in the same tiny boardinghouse—where Greene had contracted it, forty years before; he'd tried to befriend the writer's friends, to draw close to his family, even taken on Graham Carleton Greene, the writer's nephew, as his literary agent. And yet, by the end of his life, he seemed only to have become Greene the figure of tormented self-doubt. He has spent the last twenty-eight years of "continuous reflection," he writes, more than once, at the end of his 2,218-page biography, trying to catch a man who, he now realizes, will always remain outside his grasp; instead of living out his own final years, he's tried—and failed—to relive someone else's.

"You're not writing a biography?" Mike now asked.

"Oh no. The opposite. A counterbiography, as it were. I don't think you find someone by going to where he lived, least of all someone as shifting and undomesticated as Greene. I'm interested in the things that lived inside him. His terrors and obsessions. Not the life, as it were, but what it touched off in the rest of us."

"It's difficult," said Mike, tactfully. "He's a hard person to pin down."

∴

If you knew where to look, I thought, it wasn't hard at all to find him; Greene would always reveal himself with an almost desperate openness if only he could find a cover. It was his confessional impulse that led him to become a novelist, I'd generally assumed—to give us the equivalent of the dreams (sometimes fictional) he spun out for his psychoanalyst as a boy; and to work out some of the tangles he could not easily speak about in life. One may get drawn in, even spellbound, by a mystery, but one felt close only to someone one could think of as a friend.

One of the earliest books he'd written—an odd enterprise on which to waste so much energy at the beginning of a novelist's career, with finances uncertain—was a biography of the bad-boy seventeenth-century poet Lord Rochester he'd completed in his late twenties, though it was rejected then and came out, with a nice irony, only when Greene was in his late sixties. I could see why the book was turned down when I read it in my own late twenties; the prose was workmanlike and flat, and about the life of a famously satirical, silver-tongued and rakish courtier who died, as the young Greene put it mournfully, "of old age at thirty-three," apparently converting to Christianity just before he did so, Greene had made nothing but an uninflected recitation of facts.

But when I picked it up now, I realized that it didn't have to tell us much about Lord Rochester; it told us more than enough about the young Graham Greene. And even more about the person he perhaps intuited he would become. Infidelity, he wrote, only recently married himself, "tormented Rochester's conscience"; the poet of licentiousness knew that "the whole system of religion, if believed, was a greater foundation of quiet than any other thing whatsoever." But, Greene wrote, the poet's "twisted, passionate, metaphysical" mind prevented him from ever accepting it. Greene might almost have been writing parts of his own obituary in advance. "Life has somehow to be lived," he'd written, "and Rochester drank to make it endurable; he wrote to purge himself of his unhappiness;

he tried to supply artificially the adventures which no longer came to him in war and acted the innkeeper and astrologer; he flung himself, the better to forget the world, into those two extremes, love and hate."

I'd never drunk; I never felt the need to escape unhappiness or bring new drama into my life. But I knew how this kind of identification could work and how it was only through another, sometimes, that you could see yourself with shocking clarity. A real father is too close for comfort, or your vision is too clouded in trying to see what of him is in you and what in you is just a reaction against him. But a chosen father was essentially the way you—or I at least—could look long and hard at the way school had prepared us for the world but not for the domestic sphere; at how the search for truth could keep one much more engaged than accepting the finality or totality of any one position; at how the part of one that wished to be helpful also, always, feared the burden of obligation, as Mike had put it, and intrusions on one's sacred privacy.

It made no sense at all for Greene to leave off novel writing to spend all this time on a biography of a pornographic poet, except that it was a way, perhaps, for him to rebel against what he was afraid of becoming (a successful commercial writer). It was a way of asserting himself as a would-be good-for-nothing even though he had taken a wife, new responsibilities, a God into his life. It was a way of allowing H. Tench some air, still, the chance to wreak havoc and speak for the night side of things, even as he never denied the presence of the good. Greene seemed to distrust, more than anything, the sense that he (or we) might use belief or faith as a way to pretend we didn't have demons.

What gives Greene's Rochester rare poignancy and power, in fact, is that, with every sin and at every moment of his self-dynamited and errant life, the poet had a woundingly keen alertness to what he was letting down. "I myself have a sense," he wrote—and Greene highlights this—"of what the methods of my life seem so utterly to contradict." He never lost his faith in kindness, even if he could not come to belief as a whole, and "to be half kind," he wrote in one letter, "is as bad as to be half witted." His tragedy was not so much that he was a sinner as that he could always see what he could have become, the possibility of something better. "I know he is a Devil," his friend Etherege had written in a play—and Greene quotes it more than once—"but he has something of the Angel yet undefac'd in him."

∴

Greene would not be surprised if I told him that he'd written his own life story—the only searching and revealing memoir he did write—when he was in his twenties, and thinking he was completing a biography of a man long dead. He had a clearer sense than almost anyone of his class and world of all the ways the subconscious is in tune with not just what's happened, but what's to come and can write in fiction in 1938 of "the Indo-China Problem," as if knowing that it will be a headline fifteen years later, or could invent in February 1934 a dead woman found in a railway station only for a dead woman to be found in a British railway station four months later. Writing for Greene was always a form of self-examination akin to talking out one's dreams. It was also the reason that he could never dismiss religion, much though his rational mind might want to.

As a boy of five, he'd dreamed one night of a ship going

down; he awoke to learn that the *Titanic* had sunk during the night. Twelve years later he dreamed again of a boat sinking, this time in the Irish Sea; a few days later, he learned that a boat had gone down that very night, as he was sleeping, in the Irish Sea. At least two of his novels arose directly from dreams, and the last book he produced was a record of his dreams, collected in diaries when young and for twenty-four years at the end of his life and meticulously indexed (he dreamed of meeting Jean Cocteau and Ho Chi Minh, of walking through the world of the Gospels). One reason he always sought to spend the night alone was so that he could read what he'd written that day, just before he slept, and then, while he was dreaming, the "pre-conscious," as he called it, could work on the material as an outsourced accountant in Bangalore might, so that he would awaken with his narrative problems solved overnight.

That he was tapping into the future in this way was often a source of terror: he dreamed of V-1 rockets flying over London during the war and then, not long thereafter, the unmanned planes really were descending in droves. After his main character Scobie, so similar to his maker in his predicament, torn between responsibility to a wife he mostly pities and a mistress he doesn't love, takes his own life in *The Heart of the Matter,* Greene's wife, and no doubt the man himself, worried that he might be foretelling his own future. He always had a mediumistic gift, the spiritualist wife of his boyhood psychiatrist remembered in her nineties; writing, he would sink so deep into his characters that he would actually dream their dreams.

I knew how this worked from the hours I'd put in at the desk; there was no magic in the process, but there was certainly mystery. I wrote about a couple similar to one in life, but ended my book with the couple apart; as soon as the advance galleys of that work arrived on my doorstep, the couple, who had seemed very close in life, separated. I decided, one spring, to deliver my next book to my editor on September 12, 2001, before heading back to Japan; as the planes flew into the World Trade Center on September 11, I could not follow the drama that was unfolding because I was busy proofreading my novel about Islam and its quarrel with the West.

Sometimes my father would pick up a stranger's hands and read her fortune by looking at the lines on her palm; I silently looked away and assumed that this was what foreigners wanted of the "mystic East." But years later Louis told me that his mother had said that my father had seen things in her hand that no one else could possibly have known; one day, my father stopped in the middle of a reading and refused to go on, and the young woman so eager to hear about her future ended up throwing herself over a bridge, disappointed in love, six months on.

Growing up in a household with so rich and vibrant a sense of spirits spooked me at times, so I took shelter in the robust skepticisms of school; I was more than happy to close the door on forces I knew I couldn't control. But travel itself is a journey into the limits of your knowledge, as every truly alien culture shows you, sometimes terrifyingly, lines of power you'd never guessed at. In Haiti, Greene's protagonist sees the loyal soul who's become his only companion in his empty hotel suddenly turn into something else and release something dark and atavistic, primal, in a voodoo ceremony; in Kenya, during the Mau-Mau Rebellion, the very person many a Brit had taken as his faithful and all-knowing Jeeves began to "drink on his knees from a banana-trough of blood," as Greene had it, and enjoy "sexual connection with a goat." And if you credit such bush devils and Catholic voodooists—this is of course at the heart of Greene's work—then it becomes impossible to write off the Holy Ghost.

It sometimes seemed that Greene was never able to discount the existence of God precisely because he believed so fervently in the existence of His shadow. From a very early age, he'd had an unusually keen sense of evil, and story after story, through his life, shows young boys driven by a motiveless malignity who are capable of doing almost anything. That's one reason why even his most drifting characters cannot erase an image of goodness, or a code of some kind of virtue, from their heads. It doesn't stand to reason that there could be shadow without light.

∴

One day, when I was in my early thirties, someone gave me a letter he'd found from my father. My father had never been a great correspondent—speaking, being public, was his medium—but he'd sent me blue Air Letters, twice folded, when I was away at school, full of moral advice and philosophical reflection; once, when I'd stolen into a house for teachers and placed an international collect call to my parents from a phone there, dramatically wheezing into the receiver as if an obscene phone caller, he'd flown all the way over the Atlantic to rescue me from a place that could set off such a seeming bout of asthma. But he'd always remained curtained from me—he was not a writer, who puts his fears and doubts down on the page—and when I read the letter, pleading with a close friend he felt slipping away, it was as if the curtain had been torn back.

It went on for eighteen pages in all, in his small, racing hand, and I could tell from the fluency, the fervor pulsing through it, that it had been written in one sitting. As ever, there were no crossing-outs or hesitations, but there were postscripts scribbled along the margins, and afterthoughts, additions, new arguments written in at the bottom of many pages. The P.S.'s alone went on for six or seven pages at the end.

I didn't know what to do with the letter when I was done; I put it away in a closet, but the mystery of it was still inside our house, pulsing, breathing. It felt like coming into a space to see precisely the person you'd never see otherwise, because he's alone and lost in thought. I'd never known my father to plead like this, to berate, to summon forces of threat and a kind of prayer. Suddenly, he was very human—far from the commanding figure on stage with words for everything—and came to seem, wounded, less public inspiration than something very close to home.

CHAPTER 14

Greene's books are nearly all haunted by fathers: the fathers a boy has lost, and the engaging crooked adventurers who suddenly arrive on the scene and present themselves as shadow fathers of a kind. The boy on the run in his first published novel recalls the day his errant father visited him at school and talked to the headmaster; the boy on the run in his last published novel, brought out sixty years later, is abruptly visited in school, and taken from his headmaster, by a likable rogue who claims to have won the boy in a backgammon game from his real father, or the "Devil" (as he's known throughout the story).

I was taking a trip one summer around the sites of the Holy Land with my mother, and when we stopped at Sorrento, she went off to see the ruins of Pompeii, while I took a boat to Capri. I caught a bus at the port—so crowded I found myself breathing into a stranger's shirt—up to the little village of Anacapri; when I went into a money changer's booth there (I could see nothing like an information office) and said, "Villa Rosaio," the shopkeeper looked bewildered. I said it again, and suddenly he understood. "Il Rosaio!" He scribbled off a little map, leading through a labyrinth of whitewashed passageways and out of the village to an even smaller settlement, ten minutes away. As I followed his marks, footsteps falling away, at last I came to a modest house behind a gate where the local Lion's Club had put up a plaque honoring the *"cittadino onorario di Capri"* Graham Greene.

There was no mention of his books, but I thought of the tiny room on the top floor furnished only with a rough bed, a wooden trestle table, a crucifix and a skylight; for more than forty years, this had been his favorite place to write, and he'd written parts of all his later works here.

Not far away, in a bookshop, I chanced to pick up a volume that contained two short film treatments that had been properly published only after Greene's death, and when I read the second, "The Stranger's Hand" (taken from one of the magazine competitions asking for a parody of Greene that Greene himself had won), it was to find as desolate a piece as I have read, although it was about nothing more than the longing for a protector, or a friend.

A boy is deposited alone, on a plane, by his aunt—his mother is long gone—and arrives in a huge room in a Venice hotel, where he is meant to meet his father. The older man gets waylaid by a vicious wartime plot, and the little boy, who hasn't seen his father in nearly three years, starts walking and walking through the maze of the city, trying to locate the man. All he knows is that the older man has a limp and a clean-shaven face; if he sees him, he thinks, he may not even recognize his own parent.

It is a piercing picture of bereftness. The boy decides to look through every seventh doorway, he changes step every thirteen paces, he crosses two fingers to try to magick his father back to him. But Venice, so often seen as a city of lovers, is here a "city of strangers," and the boy wanders and wanders, as one hour after another passes, and people keep asking him, "Where is your mother?" His policeman father (we know, but he does not) has been literally paralyzed in a murderous political operation on the other side of town.

It could be one of the dreams that Greene published in his final book (growing up, he would sometimes imagine he had been deserted by his family). A waiter appears and plays a game with the boy, to keep him occupied.

"Will they find my father?" the boy asks. "The waiter said, 'There is always hope.' It was the most hopeless thing he could say."

Even at eight, Greene coolly notes of the boy, "one knew that all endings were not happy." A few hours later, the waiter says, "Things are not so bad if you have a friend."

The whole story might have been a parody of Greene, a skeptic would say: the quest, certain to be vexed, for a father, a Father; the man entangled in some murky world of violence in the shadows; the somewhat untrustworthy stranger who arrives to play father to the lost boy. And, of course, the friendship that results: friends are the only refuge Greene characters can turn to, and they cling to strangers even as they know that, in most cases, they are not to be trusted, or will be spirited away as soon as they are. "The Stranger's Hand"—extended in kindness (or in threat?)—could be the title for much in the emotional landscape of Graham Greene.

I didn't have to think of myself, as I read the story, arriving, three times a year, alone at a faraway airport, to go to a school where I would be (more or less happily) imprisoned for seventy days, or eighty-four. I wasn't usually in search of anything then and felt quite content stretching out on a plastic molded chair at Heathrow, using my huge suitcase as a pillow. I knew I could take the movement between places, my own company, my friendships as home. But it did make me think again of the fathers we choose, sometimes even from books, over the ones that we inherit. Real fathers, unlike conscripted ones, sometimes misplace their sons and then spend all their lives wondering how they can ever get them back.

Parents make promises in Greene—they even make prayers, as often as lovers do—and tell God they'll give up their faith if only He will spare an innocent; the one time a mother plays a prominent part in the novels, she is taken, throughout the book, to be an aunt. There are not many siblings in his fictional world, and his protagonists rarely have sons; one character who does is the hangdog detective in *The End of the Affair*, and he has the sad task of introducing his little boy Lancelot (who was meant to be called "Galahad," after the questing knight) to all the adulteries and dirty secrets of the world.

Sometimes the man will have a daughter who (as in *Our Man in Havana*) is much more grown-up, more capable and well connected than he is, even if she's only sixteen. Another of the most conspicuous daughters in Greene's work belongs to the renegade priest in *The Power and the Glory*; but the little girl seems to hate her father—plus, she's an embodiment of his mortal sin—and every time he draws close to her, she shrieks, "Don't touch me."

Yet the priest's predicament, as with so many fathers in Greene, is that he loves her even if that love is certain to destroy him. In *The Heart of the Matter* Greene's alter ego Scobie cross-questions a fat and teary Portuguese captain

coming into port (much as Greene had had to do in life, realizing that he'd never have the heart to be a policeman). He's
found a letter hidden in the captain's toilet, to his "little money
spider," promising to be good, but expressing his devotion
to his daughter in such sensual terms—"If only I could feel
your fingers running across my cheek"—that he might have
been writing to a young lover. The confusion between the
two ensures there'll always be even more to unsettle every
Greenian soul, and the people all around them.

∴

Our cruise continued—Jerusalem, Nazareth, Patmos, the
cave from which the Book of Revelation was said to have
issued—and sometimes I thought how the fathers who create
us are much harder to forgive than the ones we create, in part
because they're much harder to escape from. I would seldom
listen to anything my father said—he, after all, was the one
it was my destiny to grow away from; though if I'd heard the
same thing from someone else, or read it in a book called *Our
Man in Havana*, I'd have taken it as wisdom, as I always did
when someone told me something I probably knew already.

"I'm interested in how one can feel closer to someone one's
never met than to those one's known all one's life," I told
Hiroko when she asked what I was up to. "Why do I feel he
understands me as nobody I've met in my life can do? Why do
I feel that I understand him, as none of his other readers quite
do? How can I know, reading one of his books, what his protagonist will say and do, word for word, pages before he says or
does it?" Blood relations are not always the closest ones.

I'd picked up, on my way to the boat, the late novel of Greene's, *The Captain and the Enemy*, which I'd raced through and thrown down in a fit of disappointment when it had come out, twenty years before. I was barely out of my twenties then, busily trying to write my own destiny, and if there was one thing I had no interest in, it was fathers—and sons. Now, though, when I picked it up, I was back with the stranger's hand extended once again.

A boy is raised by his aunt, his mother long dead. He is taken from his divinity classroom by the "Captain" and set up in a shabby room next to a basement, with an ambiguous young woman he's told to treat as a mother. The minute he's in the company of the charming but obviously untrustworthy con man, he feels as if he's on his way to "the romantic city of Valparaiso," the valley of paradise. When the Captain asks the boy if he misses his mother, Jim (once Victor) says, "Not really."

"Mother is just a generic term," the Captain says hopefully.

The boy's true father is a criminal, too, we learn—"a bird of passage," in his own elusive phrase—who occasionally visits his son in his "semi-detached house" and claims to have lost him in a game of chess, not backgammon (the pedantry about the small detail itself a kind of obituary). The Captain, meanwhile, trains his eager young acolyte in all the skills of an undercover life—how to sign chits for bills you'll never pay, how to change your name according to the occasion, how, in effect, to practice a kind of fiction making in life. Then, much later, he disappears to Panama, where the boy goes to seek him out.

The Captain's final secret—I thought of Louis and our schoolboy code—is that he's been flying missions on behalf of the oppressed; he's not, ultimately, after gain or even escape, just clandestine acts of conscience. His criminal secret is that he's selfless. He's keenly aware of his responsibilities to the woman he loves and the boy he's abducted, even as he flies away from them again and again, saying that not being there is how he can best protect them.

∴

In life Greene was, by his own reckoning, a very poor parent, leaving his children effectively fatherless. In his final days, he let his daughter Caroline care for him—he had earlier bought her a thousand-acre ranch in Canada with the profits from the movie sale of *The Quiet American*. But he had never been so kind to his son, Francis, let alone their mother, and with the relatives he'd acquired through marriage most of all he lived in that peculiarly Greenian limbo of betraying them daily and being self-aware enough to feel the cost of that betrayal every hour. It's strange to recall how, in his first novel, he gives the same name to a loose woman he will soon give in life to his infant daughter, and the same name to a troubled fugitive he'll later give to his son. "That's the only subject I've got," says a sculptor who works on a huge statue of God in Greene's play, *Carving a Statue*, while his son keeps asking about the death of the boy's mother. "My indifference and the world's pain."

His father was a headmaster, readers sometimes said, so of course he was always trying to run away from those who administer punishment, on earth as much as in Heaven. But the more interesting thing about the father, according to Greene's biographers, was that he remained so dangerously innocent and trusting in men's goodness; his wife, when reading books to him, was wont to censor novels (even those written by their son). A boy is always determined to set himself apart from innocence, the more so as his elders tell him, wistfully, that it's his innocence that saves him.

When very young, Greene loved to devour boys' adventure stories about explorers and spies, which later, as a writer, he would in some respects re-create, though always with a troubled heart beating beneath the fast-moving drama. Yet as he came of age, he enlisted a literary father—to go with the shadow brother who was Lord Rochester—who could not have been further from a simple child's sense of right and wrong.

The first four pieces in Greene's *Collected Essays*—after a piece in childhood—are all about Henry James, and it is a James that few of us have seen, before or since. The novelist known for his fascination with social intricacies and psychology, for the young Greene (who wrote the two central essays between the ages of twenty-seven and thirty-two), has "a sense of evil religious in its intensity." He is preoccupied with "failure," "treachery" and "lies." A man most of us thought was writing about the complex mating dance of New World and Old—no alien theme to Greene—was, for Greene alone, writing novels that "are only saved from the deepest cynicism by the religious sense."

It was as if Greene was fashioning himself again through the man within his head. "We must always remain on our guard when reading these prefaces," he writes of the introductions to his fiction that James dictated in later life, "for at a certain level no writer has really disclosed less." Graham Greene, however, comes very close in the introductions to his early books he published only a few years after that sentence.

"You cannot render the highest kind of justice if you hate," he asserts, somehow using James's stories as the crucible for his own central code. "To render the highest justice to corruption, you must retain your innocence: you have to be conscious all the time within yourself of treachery to something valuable."

I thought back to what the English novelist had said in his early sixties to an interviewer. "One may have outgrown one's own father," he suddenly volunteered, "but one still likes to feel there's somebody there."

∴

All the time I was growing up—was it sailing into Port Said that brought this back to me? I'd last been here at the age of two, on my way to India for the first time—my father pressed only two books in my hands that I can remember well. He had more than thirteen thousand on his shelves—we had to build a hut on the hillside under our yellow home to house the overflow—and he was always ready to refer his spiritual children, as I thought of them, his students, to some high work of philosophy or the spiritual quest. But with me it was as if he was offering more worldly and more practical counsel; I could never understand why he gave me *Cards of Identity*, the antic 1950s satire of postwar Britain (though I was amused, decades later, to find that its author, Nigel Dennis, had been a writer for *Time* and a friend of the Greenes', and had taken Vivien out in New York once, after her husband left her alone in their hotel room).

Now, however, when I thought back to the eccentric story of class divisions and manufactured personalities, I could see how it might appeal to the bright-eyed imp in my father, as to his fascination with the secrets of identity. A group of quasi-psychiatrists sits in a country house, idly assigning selves—and constantly shifting names—to the patients in their care. The result is that people change guises so often you can't begin to see who they are. "Often a man is most himself when he least appears to be," says a Mr. Paradise, near the beginning of the book. Towards its end, the novel suddenly flies into a fifty-eight-page pastiche of Shakespeare:

Our play's a riddle in which ours display
The guises which your living selves portray;
The many semblances that make one you,
Shall play, through us, the game of who is who.

I didn't know why my father gave me *The Summing Up*, by Somerset Maugham, either; I read it at nineteen and felt I was listening to some high-toned godfather in a smoking jacket, telling musty stories from his armchair in a London club. As I began to travel, though, I came to take Maugham with me more and more often; no one, other than Greene, had so thoughtfully mocked conventional, too-simple morality, shown the follies of old-school British chivalry, given voice to all the passions, romances and visions that do not fit into our Boy Scout handbooks. And I never met a writer more driven by a genuine, ravenous philosophical curiosity about the human heart, the world and, in fact, the very nature of good and evil. He had, I recalled, a statue of Kuan Yin, the Buddhist goddess of compassion, on display in his hall in Cap Ferrat; he read metaphysics every morning before breakfast as some people do yoga. There was always a spiritual hunger in Maugham that

he made plausible and compact by the feline realism he never
entirely let go of.

Such books often seemed the most reliable companions
my father ever found; he would sit in his blue chair, our cat
squeezed next to him, thrumming his long fingers excitedly on
its arms, sometimes with an intensifying raga playing behind
him, and stay there all night, underlining passages in red,
scribbling one-line responses along the margins, inscribing, in
black letters that could look like Arabic, adjectives and esoteric
signs. For all his love of the public world, his deepest passions
were always very private. Three days after he died, I took *The
Summing Up* to a quiet stretch of land north of Santa Barbara
and, a set of train tracks beside me, and then the wide-open
sea, read Maugham's retrospective again, noticing for the first
time how many of his ideas, their romanticism given fiber by
their obvious shrewdness, took me back to Greene.

Fourteen years later, I found myself in Varanasi, on my
first trip to the spiritual heart of Hinduism, and a friend in
Santa Barbara gave me the name of an old friend and teacher
he suggested I look up. The professor had been his mentor
at Harvard, decades before, my friend told me, and now, in
retirement, had returned to his ancestral home near the Ganges, for half of every year, to deepen his studies and complete
a few more works of scholarship. He spoke for an old world
of literature and courtesy not often encountered in the West
anymore. I went to visit the professor one evening—we sipped
lime juice in the echoing, mostly empty high-ceilinged house,
where generations of pandits had come to visit—and after
dinner he began to recite for me the opening three books of
Paradise Lost, which he had by heart. "Of Man's First Disobe-
dience, and the Fruit / Of that Forbidden Tree, whose mortal
taste / Brought Death into the world . . ."

He grew up in an age in which boys were taught to commit thousands of lines to memory, he explained; it was a way of sharpening the mind—and of incorporating into your being the wisdom that had sustained your fathers and grandfathers, and generations before.

Then he asked a little more about me, and when I mentioned Santa Barbara, and parents who were philosophers, a fond light came into his eyes.

"I knew your father, you know."

"No!"

"Years ago, sixty years ago now. We were students together at the same small school in Bombay. He was our absolute idol. The brightest star in our solar system. We used to go over to his house just to listen to him talk."

"You must remember my grandmother, too? My uncles and aunt?"

"No," said the professor, a little apologetically. "We had eyes only for your father. He was always so generous to us. You must have known this. We were just young fools, two or three years younger than he was. But he was always so patient with us, always had time.

"I remember once he told us we just had to read this obscure new book he'd recently discovered!" The professor, now seventy-seven, smiled and lit up again at the faraway memory. He let the old title roll off his tongue. *The Road to Xanadu.* By John Livingston Lowes. About a professor of Chaucer who stumbles upon a line somewhere that reminds him of something in 'The Ancient Mariner' and then finds how some image that Coleridge had met in a poem mixed with another line he'd got from somewhere else, and then with a footnote he'd found in some other work, and they'd all coalesced in his head while he was dreaming."

"Really?"

"He was always in touch with works that sounded very obscure to us, but could change our lives."

I didn't know quite how to tell him how, that very morning, jet-lagged and seated at the guest relations desk in the lobby of the Taj Ganges Hotel, taking care of e-mails while other early risers headed out into the fog to see dead bodies floating down the river at dawn, I'd received a message from a small publishing house in New York, asking me to write a few sentences on some little-known book that everyone should read.

Without a thought, I'd started writing about the book I'd so proudly discovered in college, a secret talisman now for thirty years. *The Road to Xanadu*, by Livingston Lowes. Would I have loved it so if I'd known how much it meant to my father? It was like hearing, from my mother, three days after he died, that my father's favorite poem, which she asked me to read at his memorial service, was Yeats's "When You Are Old," the same relatively obscure poem (I had thought) I had recited for years to new companions.

CHAPTER 15

T he wind, too perfectly, picked up and the sky began to
grow dark as I pulled at last into Berkhamsted on the
local train from London Euston, continuing to Tring
and Leighton Buzzard. The day before had been a glorious,
anomalous, eighty-six-degree summer fantasy, but now it was
blowy and close to rain and the low English sky had turned
grey, even imprisoning, by the time I got out of the train. I
had never consciously sought out a Greene location before—
the trip to Capri was something I'd stumbled into—but I had
a day free in London and somehow, as never before, I felt the
presence and proximity of all those birds and bats and other
swarming terrors he'd felt around him in his ancient hometown, not far away.

Outside the small station ran green fields and a narrow road
leading up to a small bridge. I asked after the school and was
directed to the left and down a grey lane that seemed to be
called Castle Street (I remembered all the haunted men called
Castle in Greene's books, including the one in *The Human
Factor* who leads his son around the "forgotten hiding-places

and the multiple dangers" of Berkhamsted Common). Just after Castle crossed Chapel Street, the black, heraldic gates of Berkhamsted School loomed up on my right.

I had known what I would find here just by drawing on old memories: long, empty playing fields, grey plaques and chapels with locked black doors at their entrances; the cloisters would echo with the sound of my lonely footsteps. I might have been returning to one of my schools off the plane from California, four hours earlier than everyone else, thirty-five years before. At the tail end of a long summer holiday, the place would be an image of abandonment.

But as I walked through the gates now, I found the front courtyard packed: tall, tanned blond girls, in chic leggings and skirts (if only they'd been here when Greene was a student), flush with the Greek islands or villas in southern France they'd just returned from; red-faced, spotty boys, hands thrust deep into their pockets, lounging in a circle as they shot anxious glances at Old Hall and wondered whether to go in there now or whether to brave it out a little longer; a couple of mothers fussing around little Amanda or Graham, while their charges cast wistful looks at the groups of classmates not so parentally encumbered.

It was the kind of timing I'd never have believed in a novel: I had arrived at 9:55 a.m. on Thursday, August 20, and, quite by chance, 10:00 a.m. on Thursday, August 20 was the day when A-level results were being announced, essentially telling the school's departing students what the rest of their lives would be. I remembered the terror that attended these national school-leaving exams when I was a boy: how you did in them determined which college you could go to—if you could go to college at all—and what destiny, what life might await you.

The kids—they looked so grown-up now, especially with the stylish girls around (almost as if they were in a private school in a place called Hope Ranch)—headed, one by one, through the imposing door that leads to Old Hall (I strolled in behind them and saw large portraits of the school's head-masters on the walls, most prominent among them a stiff-shouldered and bespectacled Charles Greene). A minute or two later they emerged, as from their interview at St. Peter's Gate. Some athletic-looking girls with blond ponytails were jumping up and down, hugging one another, pushing away tears of joy that smeared their mascara; another girl walked over to an ax-faced mother, who tried to keep very different tears out of her eyes as she led her charge over to a wooden bench, where a teacher was handing out alternative destinies.

"Dad!" cried a red-faced boy with self-cut hair—an appren-tice football hooligan, so it seemed—as he pulled a cell phone out to share the news. "It wasn't bad at all! Yes, a D and three F's." He paused. "Actually, Dad, that's pretty good. It was a very high D."

Gangs of boys were pushing one another around, anxious to show how little they cared about all this, and punching one of their number who'd dared to get a B. A small girl trudged, as into a dentist's office, through the door marked "Careers Cen-tre." "It wasn't brilliant," a brown-haired girl with pink cheeks was saying to a shyly enquiring boy; her tone of voice said it might as well have been.

I sat on a bench next to a boy who, hands shaking, began to open his envelope; another boy was rolling his finger around the inside of his cheek, as if to steady himself.

"You're not going to open it?"

"No. I'll wait." A small, studious-looking boy with a mop of black hair affected cool, and then looked around. What would he do while he waited for his future?

"Look, look, look"—a tall boy's voice went falsetto. "I got a B!"

I remembered myself at the same day of reckoning, though by then I was already on the road, traipsing around India for my summer holidays with a huge suitcase loaded down with books on Jung and carrying a new acoustic guitar, a worn cassette of Leonard Cohen's *Songs* and the faint ambition to become a darker-skinned Leonard Cohen, first by falling in love with a blond Nordic girl and then by pursuing dissolution and the mystical life, ideally in the same breath.

In the mornings I walked across the Oval in Bombay— cricket games everywhere, many at once, crisscrossing wildly on the worn, bald grass—past the men seated on the street, selling piles of books (*Improve Your I.Q.*, Dale Carnegie's *How to Stop Worrying and Start Living*, *Right Ho, Jeeves*), to the dark, largely unlit library at the University of Bombay, my parents' first place of higher education, where I had to make my way through a single-volume *Complete Shakespeare* to prepare for university exams back in England, while birds flapped in the roof up above and I tried not to sneeze from the dust.

In the afternoons I walked back through the commotion, glanced at *The Times of India* to see if Richard Nixon had announced his resignation yet and walked up the stairs to my room at the West End Hotel, to compose a Leonard Cohen song rhyming "stranger" with "danger" and "love" with "above." When the telegram came from England, with its row of letters, it might have been a news report from another planet.

I woke up from my memory now and looked around the

main street in the small, too-typical town—the copies of the *Berkhamsted and Tring Gazette* on sale at the newsagents, the women pushing prams past the little B and B offering "Bacon Sandwiches," the Denture Care office next to a funeral director's parlor—and felt how an amiable and well-meaning town like this could close in on one till all life was gone.

There were churches everywhere—one of them had even set up a currency-exchange counter—and the people walking past me in the grey summer morning looked as comfortable and settled in their belief as parishioners. "Please Pray for All Those who are suffering in silence and who has not gotten a voice," someone had written on a scrap of paper inside the eight-hundred-year-old Norman church, onto whose graveyard Greene's nursery had looked. When I went into the local library, a kindly worker gave me a code to become a temporary member of the community and showed me the books of local history describing this as "A Commuter's Paradise."

Yet one morning in Berkhamsted had me longing for anywhere else—even somewhere dangerous and dark—instead of the innocent treadmill the town seemed to represent. By the time I returned to the school in early afternoon—"Time and Tide Wait for No Man," intoned the motto above the school clock, not far from the Admiral House Dental Practice—all the students had dispersed again, off into their future lives, and among the arched windows and turrets, the red-brick buildings towering above lawns, bulletins told me about "The 3rd Annual Scholars and Rogues Eton Fives Tournament (Sign up with Mr. Petit or Mr. Foster)." A plaque in the cloisters, not far from the classroom called "Greene's," reminded, "Berkhamsted depends on its tradition of loyalty and simplicity and discipline."

I walked across Greene's Field, home to the school tennis courts, and came to a narrow canal, with houseboats bumping along its sides and small red-brick bridges arching over it, like a slightly roughened dream of English rural paradise. A pair of teenage lovers courted shyly on a picnic table. Another walked along the bank, too embarrassed to look at each other. Off near the station, a grey set of flats made for lonely men and the love poems they wrote—it could have been North Oxford—was guarded by a black sign, "PRIVATE ROAD," and called itself, I noticed, "Greenes Court." At the station, as I waited to escape again, an announcement intoned anxiously, and monotonously, "Stand well back from the platform edge," while rumors came in that a vessel of escape was approaching.

∴

It was always the most chilling moment of the day, akin to the night of the Angel of Death; in our third "Division," just after Chambers, as it was called (when we awaited our black-gowned teachers around the "Burning Bush"), suddenly we might hear a pair of footsteps moving very rapidly along the corridor outside, past the long lines of names of the dead, past the bulletin boards summoning us to divinity class or listing the names of those who were required to show up on Saturday night for military exercises. Something would stop in me—in all of us—and then there would come a rap on the door and it would fly open and an older boy with a "stick-up" white collar would step into the classroom.

"Is Iyer in this Division, sir?"

"Yes."

"He is to see the Head Master at eleven forty."

For drawing on Treitel's trigonometry answers, or stealing across the bridge in mufti to hear the Strawbs play in Windsor. For sins I hadn't even known were infractions.

In time—this was the logic of the system, teaching you to obey and to command, to work within a precisely determined order (all things come to pass and the young, too, shall one day grow old)—I, in turn, would become a *praepostor* (the word comes from a medieval term for a monastic prior) and start making official visitations from our local God. You had to learn how to administer hardship as well as to endure it, the system was saying; it was fine to read "Endymion" and play Mozart on the piano next to the Lower Tea Room—near-perfect recitals would float up through the stairwells to where we were doing homework, from other boys, and one teacher would earnestly show us the parallels between Keats and Joni Mitchell—but the world expected firmness, and to be wet was to be lower than the mud. There were two sins: admitting to an act of decency (indecency was prized, of course) and underestimating the toughness and complexity of the world.

One time, at the Dragon, Turpin made a run for it, slipping out of Leviathan, or whichever room several of us were sharing then, and disappearing off into the dark. Rumors ran excitedly around School House: he had been seen making his way back to his parents' house in Wales, he was heading in the other direction, across the wilds, like a character in Hardy. He had always seemed among the frailest, sniffling well into the second week of term, and now he had tried—simple folly—to take his destiny into his own hands (a scene that comes up again and again in Greene).

Within a few days, though, he was gathered in again—there

was talk of the Parable of the Lost Sheep—and back in one of
the beds in our room, squandering the glamour of his escape
by turning his back to us and sniffling away as he lay facing
the wall. In my next school, the only African student—son of
some bigwig in the Nigerian government—would do the same
and soon the tabloids would be full of this boarding school boy
who had set up a "love nest" in Chelsea with two blondes; it
was always said that boys from the school ended up in record
numbers in prison, as well as in 10 Downing Street, and sometimes professed not to see much difference between them.
One of my friends would go on to become a shaman (though,
as he wryly admitted, his license hanging on his wall, it was
hard to find clients for soul retrieval); another would man the
level-crossing gate on a rural railway line, watching it go up
and then go down again. Eighteen Old Boys had gone on to
become British prime minister and, as I write this, the nine-
teenth has just come to power, and the current Thai prime
minister, as well as the two sons of the British Crown Prince,
emerged from the same cloisters.

Such schools were famously a training ground for Empire,
so it was no surprise that British rule across the globe could be
seen as a version of school, extended to a life sentence: it was
never hard to see geopolitics (if you were Graham Greene, at
least) as an unending competition between the bullies who'd
become cabinet ministers and their painfully sensitive victims.
When he was in West Africa, his protagonist would meet a
man who blurts out "I love you" to a colleague's wife he's met
just once, when in Sweden, a smooth charmer who hopes that
his silky confidence will somehow obscure his shiftlessness.
All across the world, from Brighton to Saigon, we meet in his
books a small group of boys, tied in a kind of fellowship and liv-

ing in spartan quarters, very simply, clinging to their worn-out innocence as if they were still in the room called Pterodactyl.

You could say that he gained from school not just his schoolboy's sense of adventure, his love of mischief, his uncertainty about what to do with the most foreign country of all (the other sex), but his almost superstitious revulsion from success. In the famous book Cyril Connolly had written about our school—his "autobiography of ideas"—he'd recalled being asked to write essays on themes like "Nothing fails like success" or "Nothing succeeds like failure." Connolly's classmate, who wrote under the name of George Orwell, would say, "Failure seemed to me the only true virtue," and success a kind of bullying, or ugly imperialism. And British intelligence, of course, rose out of such hallways, which meant that it was doomed to failure, perhaps, and Greene could never take it seriously. The people we knew best, school ensured, were ones we were not related to, and the ones who knew us best, prey to our every waking secret through the formative years of our lives, might be people we'd never see again. But they lived inside our heads forever.

Decades later, as the leaves were turning all around me on a radiant autumn morning in Japan, the sky a shocking blue, I saw the witch doctors I'd first met as a teenager in Bolivia, the meal I was taking in a fisherman's hut along the Amazon, the chain-smoking ten-year-old who was leading me on horseback through the jungles of Colombia, only five months after I'd quit my cell in New Buildings, and seemingly the last part of its lifelong training.

"School was what we had instead of family," I heard myself telling Hiroko, and then looked up to see her startled face staring back at me.

∴

I was traveling alone through Sri Lanka in the summer of 2006, a time when the civil war, after three years of cease-fire, had started up again with new intensity; each day the newspapers were full of senseless killings. My first morning in the capital, as I was eating breakfast, the deputy chief of staff of the Sri Lankan army was assassinated by a suicide bomber as he drove to work a few miles away; five minutes from my hotel, the city's main hospital was barricaded behind roadblocks and signs saying "HIGH SECURITY ZONE" because, just eight weeks before, a pregnant woman had walked into a heavily guarded compound and detonated a bomb hidden in her clothing, critically injuring the army chief of staff and leaving nine others dead (among them, of course, her baby and herself).

Six sightseers in a national park had been killed, apparently by guerrillas, a few weeks earlier; a bus had passed over a mine, and sixty-four more innocents had died. After the assault on the deputy chief of staff, a rumor ran through the country that the next attack was going to be on a school. Parents, wild-eyed, raced into classrooms, brandishing swords and sticks, pulling their children out; it was said that explosives had been found inside a small boy's slippers.

I, as in a dark-framed farce, was visiting the island on the almost-comical pretext of seeing the places that Marco Polo had written about, briefly, more than seven hundred years before. I'd agreed to the assignment eight months earlier, when things were relatively peaceful, but by the time I arrived, the violence was so everywhere that the island's hotels were empty. Bellboys clustered round me every time I left my room in the silent hotel, hungry for handouts, and when I walked out onto the beach, where children flew kites and couples unpacked picnics, it was to see twenty-one soldiers standing, guns raised, under the palm trees, while helicopters whirred and circled overhead. My first weekend in the country, a journalist was gunned down three miles from where I was sipping tea.

To add to the unsought horror, it was Tamils, people with names such as Iyer and features such as mine, who were at the heart of the war, as they agitated for their independence from a Sri Lanka that saw itself as the Buddha's chosen land. Everyone was jumpy, braced for the next explosion, and I was left counting the days till I could be gone; I watched little boys ride ponies on Galle Face Green and retreated in the evenings to the deserted bar in my hotel to see Britain play Portugal in the World Cup on TV.

On the southern coast of the island, always quiet, and around the area where a tsunami less than two years before had carried away thirty-six thousand Sri Lankans to their deaths—the sleepy, palm-fringed, two-lane road by the ocean was lined with fresh white crosses—I was looking for who knows what (I'd discovered by now that in all likelihood Marco Polo had never been to "Zeilan" at the time he committed his eight paragraphs on it) when I noticed it was lunchtime. There was not an abundance of possibilities among these villages doubly empty since the storm, but my taxi driver assured me that he knew just the place. We turned off the narrow road, down an unmarked lane and, bumping through the jungle, suddenly ended up, absurdly, at a gorgeous modernist structure, all glass walls and reflecting pools, above an empty white-sand beach.

I got out at the luxury hotel—glossy brochures told me I could rent a private villa for hundreds of dollars a night—and started walking through what might have been a cutting-edge, minimalist museum in Fort Worth. In front of me, though the place was almost empty, stood a very tall, lean figure, brown hair falling to his shoulders, in chic white cotton shirt and jeans, barefoot, hands tucked into his back pockets as he spoke to a trim Japanese in all-black designer clothes.

He turned around. "I can't believe it!" I said, almost in spite of myself. "I haven't seen you since, it must be, 1974."

"You almost gave me a heart attack," replied the French film star, as he'd seemed a second before, posing for a paparazzo shot in *Paris Match*. "What the hell are you doing here?"

We'd shared Latin classes together under C. A. Impey in Berkshire thirty-five years before—was it Ovid's *Metamorphoses* or the Punic Wars?—and now François was manager of the super-luxe hotel, having served stints opening and running hotels in Haiti, Rajasthan, Siem Reap and Java. Neither of us was as amazed as he might have been, because such sightings of old classmates were part of how our system worked, exporting the values and even the fellow prisoners of school across the globe to the point where Greene, returning from a three-day jungle patrol in Malaya, ran into the very boy (in the Cold Storage Company in Kuala Lumpur, no less) who had marked him for life with the idea of betrayal, having turned on him in school thirty years before (now, inevitably, he looked like just another "customs and excise man," fox-faced with a small mustache). Stationed in Freetown—the name itself seems to belong to allegory—working for British intelligence during the war, he had bumped into a district commissioner upcountry who proved (of course) to be an enemy of his from Oxford, unforgiving. In Nairobi, he stumbled into one of his closest friends from university, known for his dry irrationality.

François and I decided to have lunch together, and over elegant Earl Grey and Sri Lankan curries we revisited old classmates now working as greeters or columnists or con men, some of them laid low forever by drugs. I remembered the boy who had sat near me as we trudged through regimental sentences and wrote long poems in dead languages, stylish and exotic even then (the only of our students to come from France), and wondered if all of us had been trained only to occupy temporary quarters such as this, on the edge of a jungle, unaffiliated. Then I got back in my car and went back into the war.

For most of the days that followed I sat in my room, too distressed by the torpor and desperation all around to go out very much. I waited for the World Cup games in the evening. I read a novel about a man who had gone to Ecuador and come back in thrall to a drug that made him live in the realm of fantasy. The sea washed against the beach outside my window and the palm trees bent in the violent wind.

My last day in Sri Lanka, I decided to contact Lasantha Wickrematunge, the local journalist who was *Time's* man in Colombo and, as editor of the local *Sunday Leader*, was accustomed to briefing colleagues from abroad. He suggested we meet at the Taj—it offered a lavish buffet on Sundays—and, as we sat in the empty restaurant, waiters hovering around us, Lasantha, smiling, slightly round, in his late forties, told me about his three children, one of whom he'd named "Ahimsa," meaning "nonviolence," in direct tribute to his hero Gandhi. Armed men had attacked his home because of his truth telling, he told me; he'd been on Amnesty International's "endangered list" for eight years now. But it was his duty to stay here and tell his countrymen what was really happening, especially since he had known most of the republic's leaders so long that he might have been their brother.

I could have been listening, I thought, to one of the characters in a Greene novel—*The Comedians,* say—who calls out for conscience and bold action with a sincerity that makes one fear for him; certainly our conversation was a contrast to the rather jaded world-traveler chat, and talk of murder in Sri Lankan villages, I'd had with François earlier in the week. Lasantha had even blown the whistle on his old friend the president, and his brother, he told me now, with a pained, embarrassed grin, and a massive scam they'd been involved in. One could imagine how angry the president had been.

I was in no position to see what his own interests were in all of this, and what those who didn't admire him might have said in turn, but it was hard not to be won over by such an earnest and devoted spirit; he made journalism sound like a holy calling. Two and a half years later, when I had to go back to Sri Lanka, I made a note to myself to contact Lasantha as soon as I arrived, to see how my new friend was doing.

Sixteen days before I got to Colombo, I picked up a newspaper in Varanasi, and read that Lasantha Wickrematunge had been killed. The previous day four men on motorbikes had cut him off in his car as he drove to work and pumped him full of bullets. The president had promptly expressed his shock and called for an investigation; it wasn't impossible that someone had committed the heinous act, he said, to put his government in a bad light.

Three days after that, however, another article appeared, reprinted from Lasantha's own paper (and quickly picked up in almost every country across the globe). It was an article Lasantha had written before his assassination, in which he wrote, calmly, about his impending death and laid it at the president's door. "When finally I am killed," he had written, "it will be the government that kills me." At one point he had even addressed the president, his old friend, directly. "In the wake of my death I know you will make all the usual sanctimonious noises to call upon the police to hold a swift and timely inquiry. But like all inquiries you have held in the past, nothing will come of this one, too. For truth be told, we both know who will be behind my death, but dare not call his name."

The piece was called "And Then They Came for Me," after a line by the German theologian Martin Niemöller, who had once been an admirer of Hitler's but then had left the cause and seen its ministers of death gradually expand their net, coming first for the Jews, and then the Communists, and then the trade unionists and finally (because there was no one left to protect him) for him, taking him to the camps where he was incarcerated for eight years. Lasantha's wife took over his newspaper, but within a few weeks she was driven out of the country, fearful for her life. Sri Lanka's narrow country roads were crowded with billboards when I drove down them again, showing grinning soldiers brandishing guns and crying for "Victory" as the government launched its final attack on the guerrillas in the north, leaving up to forty thousand Tamil civilians dead and as many as three hundred thousand others dispossessed.

"Greeneland perhaps," as the man had written, rather wearily, of a world that some claimed existed merely in his imagination. "I can only say it is the land in which I have passed much of my life."

CHAPTER 16

I f you grow up between cultures, if you get accustomed to
traveling, it's easy to find yourself always on the outside
of things, looking in. This can be ideal for a writer—or a
spy; you've always got, analytically, a ticket out. You can see
England through the questing, impatient eyes of California,
see California as it might look to someone from England, dangerously up in the air, unformed, unformalized. You can be
satirist or romantic and use what you see for any purpose at
all. But if you're honest with yourself—and my Greene was, to
a humbling degree—you have to take the measure of what's
lost when you're not committed.

That's why, over and over, the older male characters in his
books find themselves alone, in a kind of vacuum; the young
boys in his stories, by contrast, dream of becoming adventurers, taken up by dashing rogues, given a script of sorts, working
in clear-cut terms for good or even mischief. That's one thing
the older men cannot forgive: there's innocence in belief, however mistaken, and hopeful illusions are sometimes the only
way we can make our peace with life.

It wasn't because of Greene that I began spending time in a Catholic monastery; if anything, it was in spite of him. No one had written more pitilessly of the hollowness of mere piety and the difference between a good act and a good man; no one had shown more sharply how rarely one leads to the other. And growing up in a house where so many were speaking of mystical transcendence had probably made me more skeptical than I might otherwise have been of what my deepest nature prompted me towards. If anything of real substance or value were to be found, I thought, it could come only in the middle of the very real world and a chaos like Colombo's. Mere tolling bells and silent cloisters—men in gowns singing psalms— could not have much effect on someone who's put in years in British boarding school.

But a friend who taught at a high school in Santa Barbara told me that he took his classes to the monastery every term, and he was amazed to see how even sixteen-year-old Californian schoolboys were cleaned out and rendered silent by the days in silence. The terminology, the doctrine, the Catholic apparatus weren't important, my (non-Catholic) friend said; but in a place of quiet you could better see what you cared about and leave behind the self that usually smothered and entrapped you like a winter coat.

I drove up through the mountains—my mother and I were staying in a temporary apartment as our house was slowly rebuilt after the fire the year before—and then along the sea, passing elephant seals sleeping on the beach and lonely lighthouses above the rocks, great empty meadows rolling down to the ocean. Then I turned right at a high wooden cross and started to wind around the curves of an even more twisty road. Along the way I saw benches, empty, set out around every turn to look out on the flat Pacific and the sun scintillating on the blue-green waters.

When I got to the parking lot, a monk led me to a small room and I found a wide desk in front of a huge window, looking out on a small walled garden, a white chair in front of a splintered wooden fence. Beyond that was a slope, running down between coastal live oaks and eucalyptus trees, towards the ocean. It sat before me in the winter afternoon—not a ship or island to be seen—and I realized that, from where I sat, I could not see a single human habitation. Only a blue jay alighting on the fence outside, a rabbit scuttling into the undergrowth, the still blue plate of the sea far below.

I sat down and began to write, though I had nothing to write about, I'd thought. Words poured out of me, in spite of me, pages of them, and I transcribed them as rapidly as if they were love letters aimed at nothing but the world around me. Bells tolled outside, and I guessed the white-hooded monks and their other nine visitors were gathering in the chapel. Bells tolled again, and I realized they were assembling in the rotunda for silent meditation. The sun began to disappear behind a ridge, and then colors, wild but more silent somehow than they would be in our own hillside home down the coast, began to line the sky.

Darkness fell, and still I was writing. Words of radiance and affirmation that might have come from some unfallen self inside me I'd all but forgotten. When finally I got up, it was seven thirty—four and a half hours had passed—and I hadn't begun to unpack my carry-on.

Very quickly, I found that the hermitage was as exciting and alive a place as I had seen, and coming there at least as great an instruction and adventure as going to Bolivia or Cuba or even Ethiopia: the place that gives the other places meaning. I came back three months after my first stay, and then four months after that (to spend the days reading Henry Miller). I came back the next spring for two weeks, and then returned a little later for three weeks. Here I could step behind the many voices I could speak in, and into a place of absolute wholeness, which is self-trust; I couldn't imagine second thoughts or mere courtesies here, and whatever instinct I followed—and that's all I did I knew at the core to be the right one.

When the fourteen guest rooms were full, the monks, with typical kindness, allowed me to stay with them in the cloister. Once I occupied a Silver Bullet trailer reserved for those who worked on the property; sometimes they put me with the monastery's workers in the two-story Ranch House, and every time I came down the creaking stairs, it was to see a monk doing chin-ups in the dusty boarding-school room, or pulling a copy of Robert Evans's roguish autobiography, *The Kid Stays in the Picture,* out of the Ranch House shelves. Sometimes, in one of the guest trailers on the hill, with the rain pouring down and not a soul or light to be seen within the fog, for day after dark day, I felt in some biblical place of terror, a wilderness. The chilling line from *The Cloud of Unknowing* came back to me: "The Devil has his contemplatives, as God has His."

I came to see how monks live with furious doubts, as any lovers do; when the rain came down, screening me from the world, I sometimes felt as alone and undefended as in a desert. I devoured Emerson and Thoreau every morning with my breakfast, though the silence itself was writing new volumes of theirs each day; then I spent long days with Melville or Cormac McCarthy, so that I could hear what thunderous challenge sounded like, too. A love affair that is all light—which is what being here felt like—is itself a kind of trick, probably put about by the dark.

One sultry day in midsummer I invited a troubled friend from down the coast to visit me in the hermitage; if anywhere could bring her calm, I thought, it would be here. As soon as I led her into the chapel, she broke into tears before the small cross suspended from a skylight in a warm, round, golden space.

"You're moved?" I said.

"Not only." I could hear what even the stillness could not heal. "I can feel all the things I never had when I was growing up. That sense of protectedness, of being held."

She might have been speaking with Greene's voice, I thought, so ambivalent about a peace that he could see, but from which he would always be excluded, usually by himself. And in any case, he would surely have added, a place of quiet can only be a hideout, a refuge from the world and its troubles, not a response to it. For a certain kind of soul, a sanctuary is precisely the place where you feel least calm, or deserving.

∴

I was never much interested in Greene the man of politics or Greene the Catholic, Greene the rumored spy, in part because I didn't think he was much interested in them, at the deepest level; all were mere symptoms of some more fundamental trembling. No one can be defined by the roles he plays onstage. I watched my neighbors in California embark on lifelong excursions into the self, while seeming baffled by the world; I saw my friends in Britain more or less take over the world, but only by never looking too closely within. Greene, I felt, was always in his books hoping to give us a sense of responsibility—of conscience—in part by bringing himself before an unsparing tribunal.

At heart he offered me a way of looking at things, and the way one looked became a kind of theology, a preparation for a way of acting. It didn't matter if the man within my head— this one at least—was carefully edited or artfully fashioned; his unearthly, unflinching blind man's eyes gave me an image of attention, and the spirit that lies behind it.

One evening I stepped into a tiny flat in Bangkok—it belonged to an Englishman I'd met only briefly—and saw a guitar by the bed, a stuffed panda nestled against the pillows, a little photo of a monastery in the Himalayas propped against the corner of one shelf. I'm not sure my new friend would ever have imagined a room like this—a room from school, really— awaiting him when he was fifty-five. A long line of books, mostly biographies and history works of an imperial cast, filled a single shelf, and next to them ten BBC videos that he pulled out for me.

In an alcove sat a computer and on its top a picture of a sweet-looking Thai girl in her twenties.

"She's the first in her family to go out into the modern world," my friend told me, with obvious pride. "Her father's a fisherman. Her degree was in English."

"Have you known her long?"

"Four years."

"Do you think you'll . . . ?"

"I'll introduce her to my mother, back in England. But I tell her—I told her father, too—that I wouldn't wish me on her.

She deserves something better. I've never—well, I mean, she's still a virgin."

Greene was the only novelist I'd heard of who prayed for the fearful creatures he'd created.

∴

I never wanted to meet Graham Greene, I often told myself; the one person in his life I'd have liked to talk to was his long-abandoned wife, Vivien, who seemed to have seen him as clearly as anyone, with just the lack of delusion that he cherished, and then had had sixty years to reflect upon this fugitive who had brought her children into the world only to haunt them with his long absences. Besides, it was Greene himself who had taught me how the author we meet can never, by definition, be quite the one we love; as soon as he's meeting us, he's looking away from his desk, putting on a public face to greet the world.

I knew how it would be if I took the train down to Antibes and then the short walk to his anonymous, modern apartment building. I'd press the button at the bottom that said "Green" (a threadbare camouflage) and he'd be waiting for me at the door as I came up. I'd ask him about the Cuban painting that Fidel had given him, hanging on the wall, and the Haitian artifacts that were the only striking things in a room that gave no hint as to his life or personality. As he made us drinks, I'd run my eye, as if surreptitiously, along the books neatly lined up on the white shelves, and when I sat down in the bamboo chair, I'd be prepared for him to disclose certain things I might take as private; offering a few secrets is how you throw people off the scent of others. I'd be muffled, deferential, not wanting to set him off with a stray, foolish reference to one of his friends, so it would be almost guaranteed that nothing real would get said.

I'd come away, of course, with a souvenir—the illusion that I "knew" him a little—but the cost would be tremendous: now I'd be distracted by the unexpectedly high voice, the erect carriage, the reddened face. I'd be further from knowing him than ever. A man within your head whispers his secrets and fears to you, and it can go right to your core; accompanied by flesh and blood, it comes up to the surface, and you're aware only of the good manners and laughter that keep you on the far side of a barrier.

∴

Winters are cold in Bhutan. I had stolen into the country, largely closed though it is, through a loophole in the immigration laws—those with Indian passports could come and stay for weeks or months, paying a tenth of the two hundred dollars a day demanded of the strictly regimented tourist—and I'd taken a room in the modest Druk Hotel, at the center of Thimphu, the capital. "Capital" is a grand word for a place without traffic lights or television; the little town of twenty thousand was one of the most silent places I'd seen, and as I sat with my mango juice at the breakfast table, I glanced outside to find men in traditional costumes—they looked like dressing gowns—walking to an empty field between the willows to practice archery.

There was little to do in Bhutan after I'd taken a car out to its distant valleys and temple-fortresses built on remote crags, and in the quiet, unfurnished days I found myself rummaging among the shelves of the tiny library in the capital for Jackie Collins books, or watching the crowds assemble for the night's Stallone movie at a cinema. A few Japanese businessmen sat anxiously around tables in the Druk dining room, but after I'd eaten dinner, there was little company to be had except for books.

I'd brought along, inevitably, my most reliable companion, and one afternoon, with nothing else to do, I opened *The Comedians*. It is a typical Greene tale—too typical, some would say—in which the main characters, Brown and Jones, are almost indistinguishable rogues, on the run, with identities they change at every moment and no real friends or family to hold them to their word. Brown lives in an empty hotel he owns in Port-au-Prince—he was born in Monte Carlo to a father he never saw and a mother of uncertain parentage—while Jones, who turns out to be partly Indian, will die "along the international road." All their lives, we're meant to assume, they're lingering on the border, neither one thing nor the other, comedians sailing into Haiti to try to turn its moral darkness to advantage.

Set against these two masters of neutrality is an earnest couple from Philadelphia, the Smiths, who are missionaries determined to make the world a purer place, quiet Americans who've grown a generation older but not up. In the savagery of Papa Doc Duvalier's dictatorship, their good intentions seem especially pitiful—until we see that their goodness and innocent conviction move them to acts of courage and righteousness that the nonbelieving Brown (picking up a diplomat's wife as his sometime mistress and mocking them as an adolescent might) can never rise to. As with many of the Americans in Greene's work, their high hopes for the world seem foolish until we see the alternatives.

This was none of it so different from what I knew already from the many Greenes I'd read. In the middle of the comedy—Jones slips into an ambassador's house dressed in women's clothes; we meet a couple of Duponts, as in a Tintin book (and, later, a prostitute called "Tin Tin"); the passengers on the good ship *Medea* blow up condoms to serve as balloons—we see that the realest thing of all is terror, which leaves no space or scope for mere detachment. "Cynicism is cheap," says Greene's cynical protagonist Brown, "you can buy it at any Monoprix store—it's built into all poor quality goods." The last words his dying mother had said to him, before leaving him the hotel, were "Which part are you playing now?"

This was all familiar enough to me. But as I flipped through the pages, with nothing to distract me—it was silent outside in the square, and the light was beginning to fade—something strange began to happen. I felt as if I was on the inside of the book, a spotlight trained on something deep inside me. Whatever questions the story was posing to Brown, about where he stood and what he'd do, it seemed to be posing to me. Why was I here, in a country with which I had no connection when I could be somewhere that had real stakes for me? Why was I not with my new love, Hiroko, in Japan, instead of collecting impressions of a place that ultimately meant little to me? Wasn't love (or faith, in fact) a matter not of feelings but of actions, and those actions measured by how many of them you'd have done without the love (or faith)?

I read and read, not noticing how deep I was getting. The winter sun began to sink behind the mountains, and it grew chill. I put on the gas heater next to the bed—two orange bars began to glow—and then I put on the lights. As the action went on, Brown's very urbanity and Englishness began to seem a crime, a sin in a world of unequivocal evil; as ever for me in Greene, the power of the story came from the stab of self-accusation. "The Church condemns violence," I read, "but it condemns indifference more harshly. Violence can be the expression of love, indifference never."

And then—this was travel, in all its tragic comedy—the lights went off. Across the country, I came to believe. I was in the dark, quite literally, except for the two rows of orange on the floor. I fumbled across the room and made out a shape that seemed to be the bedside table. There looked to be a candle there, but I had no expectation of matches, and even if there was a box somewhere, I had no way of laying my hands on it.

Outside, the town was entirely silent. Not even a honk or a shout.

The people around me were used to this, I assumed; they were plunged into darkness every other night, perhaps. There was no sound of scrabbling, or of improvised solutions. The whole country might have been waiting in a state of suspended animation.

But I was aflame, and I needed to be back in the world that had possessed me. I carried my book over to where I could see the bars of orange and sat down on the floor, to keep reading by their light. I read and read in the dark, the silence of a monastery (or a hall where students were taking some exam) around me. When I was finished, I lay on my bed and my heart thumped, thumped against my rib cage.

I didn't know what to do; it was like being in the middle of a conversation and then looking up and noticing you are alone, in a dark room, in a silent land of mountains.

I got up and stumbled across the room to a dresser, where I'd noticed there was a decorated folder with some writing paper inside it. I brought back a few yellow pages—"Druk Hotel" on them, and ornamental designs evoking the Land of the Thunder Dragon—and began, crouched on the floor next to the fire, to write. To myself? To whoever cared about my little predicament? To the name I put at the top?

Out it all came, like a confession and an essay all at once: everything the novel had made me feel as it pinned me against the wall and asked the cost of watching from the sidelines. I covered two pages, and then three more, then I scribbled across a sixth page, and put my name at the bottom.

The lights were still out for as far as I could see, and I lay on my bed, heart pounding like a gong. No dinner that night, no anything. The next morning, the sun showed up again over the hills—I heard people walking along the corridor—and, now that it was no longer needed, the electricity of course returned.

I went out into the winter morning—the cold slapped me awake after the two bars of heat in my room—and walked amidst the medieval dressing gowns and sturdy white houses built in traditional fourteenth-century style to the post office. Letters here seemed about as plausible as time capsules sent into space; in the Druk Hotel, it had been almost impossible even to communicate with the front desk. But I pulled out the address book I had in my shoulder bag and scribbled down the names I always carried with me as a talisman: "Graham Greene, Residence des Fleurs, avenue Pasteur, Antibes, France."

Then I handed the ornamental envelope over and returned to my day-to-day life.

∴

A few days later I was out of Bhutan, though still feeling naked and raw, and a few weeks later I was back in California, floating through the usual dinners and distractions that ensured I'd never have the time or space to cut beneath the surface. I might never have read the book, it would seem to somebody watching me. But something in me had turned, and I realized that wit or clever observation would never be enough. The safe position was rarely the right one.

I wondered how long I would write in hotels and what might be the price of being untied to any one culture, all the things I loved so habitually. I thought about how I could begin to rectify this and plant my feet on solid ground. But, as with any intimate conversation, especially with a stranger, these weren't reflections I could easily share. A few months later, I wrote another long letter, to the same address, telling its recipient, now eighty-five, how much I knew he valued his privacy and how well I knew all the questions he didn't like to be asked. Still, if he wanted to explain himself to *Time* magazine—he continued to write indignant letters to the magazine, and he'd sometimes written for *Life;* he'd gone out of his way to mention *Time* in *The Quiet American* and *Our Man in Havana* and *A Burnt-Out Case*—I'd be happy to serve as a cross-examiner.

A few weeks later, the little blue envelope arrived, as I knew it would, with the single sheet inside (typed for years by his sister Elisabeth), his spidery signature at the bottom. If any letter could make him succumb, he wrote, in just the courteous, elegant tones I'd expected, it would be mine. But time was short now, and he had much to do.

Months earlier, as it happened, Elisabeth had suffered a stroke, and Greene had been so devastated that he could barely look at her, I later heard, and collapsed in sobs. The old man was himself unwell, and had lost another part of himself when his closest brother, Hugh, died, two years before. Seven months later, our house burned down, and his letter, and all the thoughts I'd scribbled down of him, my plans for becoming a writer, were reduced to ash. Ten months after that, I turned on the radio one morning and heard that Graham Greene was dead.

Now our exchanges were safer—more intimate—than ever.

CHAPTER 17

My father never mentioned Graham Greene, that I can remember; he disliked Catholicism—a long-time rival to the Neo-Platonism he cherished—and rejoiced when his infant son, in the maternity ward, began to bawl every time a Catholic nun came to pray for him, setting off a room full of bawls that drove the poor sister away. Yet he had been taught, of course, by Catholics, at schools named after half-forgotten saints, and it was they who had given him *Othello* and "The Scholar Gypsy" and the English he now used so powerfully. It was they who had, indirectly, sent him to England, and I'm not sure he'd ever have had time for Englishmen like Greene, with all the "advantages," who were so determined to turn their backs on that inheritance and concentrate on the failures of Empire, the worthless and the forgotten.

They might almost have been moving in opposite directions: my father, through the innocence of his background and his unembarrassed hopes, eager to enjoy the spaciousness and history of Britain, while Greene sometimes seemed to long for nothing more than an anonymous house on the backstreets of Bombay. Both longed, as most of us do, for precisely the world they never knew, and had they met, it might have been on one of the busy streets of Piccadilly, where each would be walking towards the other's home.

Sometimes my father sent folders downstairs to me through his students: did I want to see this essay about the Golden Ratio he'd just unearthed, and would I look at and edit this lecture of his that had been transcribed? There was this new version of the Gospel according to Thomas he was putting together, and he'd got caught up in the issues of *Antigone* again. He had books on public speaking beside his eccentric cigarillos (though when he died, a member of Parliament, writing in London's *Independent,* would call him "the most eloquent, and erudite, student debater of the decade in the 1950s—or, perhaps, any other decade"); the *TLS* arrived in our mailbox even in the coyote-haunted hills of California and annual dues streamed in from the Reform Club (where Jim in Greene's last novel goes to meet his wandering father). He was a Gandhian and a vocal socialist. but he had never fully managed to wash from his head all the golden visions of England he'd been given as a boy.

He'd been generous enough to send his only son through a British educational system that would ensure—though perhaps he hadn't seen this fully in advance—that the son would have no interest in staying in Britain and no particular interest in getting ahead or having a life of settledness or public success. I'm not sure he realized quite how much the British system trains its subjects in going their own unlikely way and learning how to stand out mostly inwardly. He was delighted when Louis came to visit during the holidays, but less so, I suspected, to see his own son, as British school had taught, leaving a seemingly secure job in midtown Manhattan to live in a rented two-room cell in an anonymous Japanese suburb, with no printer or car or fast Internet connection, and only a sense of time and space that could feel like deepest freedom.

∴

One winter day, when I was barely thirty, he said to me, "There's one problem with California." I wasn't eager to listen, but the sentence had a promising beginning. "It has no understanding of evil." Did he mean that it was too innocent, unready for the world? Or only that it didn't know what to do with the dark? Certainly it had exiled history and chosen to ground itself in the future perfect, the born-again optimism of a place convinced, as even the Christian evangelists here said, that "The Future is your Friend." But when it came to ancient words or unburied spirits, to the self-delighting chicanery of an Iago, or Milton's Satan, it seemed painfully undefended, at least as those from older cultures tend to assume quiet Americans might be.

He pointed out a student of his—I'll call him Simon—who did in truth seem the very incarnation of all the boyishness and openness that so revived us in California, Billy Budd reborn. Simon would do anything my father asked: go across town to buy him a plate of chile rellenos, drive two hundred miles to collect a classmate from Los Angeles Airport. When the sleepless professor needed someone to talk to at 1:00 a.m., there would be Simon, on our doorstep. I thought of him, with his politeness, his eagerness to please, his unqualified belief in a better world and his trust in father figures, as the kind of ingenue we'd have remorselessly teased at school.

I went to Japan for a year, to get away from everything associated with a twenty-fifth-floor office and an embossed business card, living according to someone else's idea of happiness, and almost the day I came back, I was faced with a drama: Simon had gone off the rails. He'd grown tired of running errands for his professor and now he claimed he was being used as an unpaid servant. More than that, he was almost possessed in his rage; it was as if his savagery now was in direct proportion to his sweetness before. Disenchantment was common in California in those days, if only because enchantment had been so strong a few years earlier. Reality seemed so paltry next to castles—dungeons—in the air.

It was a fearful scene, and I never had time to ask my father if he thought now that California was too innocent; hearing how the loud American, Granger, he's always mocked, is in fact praying for his ill son, seeing how recklessly he's meddled in Pyle's fate, the Englishman in *The Quiet American* realizes how much he is like them, ultimately, in his inability to see things as they are. My father decided it was better to defuse the situation through absenting himself and in the months that followed, I saw him less and less often, and many times he was away for months on end.

I kept up with my life, commuting as I had done as a boy between a very young "Golden State" that offered freshness and conviction, if not wisdom, and a much more veiled, reticent, older culture (not England now but Japan) where people found their pleasure in curious hobbies, little fantasies, precisely because they assumed that the larger terms of life were given, fixed. Sometimes—often—I thought back on the Darwinian hothouse of my school days, strikingly similar in its sense of hierarchy, of stoicism and endurance, of military self-discipline, to what was around me in structured, small-scale Japan; I recalled how well it had been preparing me, effectively, for a monastery. All those Marcus Aurelius sentences we'd had to read and memorize, all the lines from *Hecuba* we'd had to recite in Greek were telling us that it wasn't the world and its trials and sufferings that made us, but our response to them. The fault was never in our stars, or even in our fathers.

The second volume of Sherry's biography came out, and as I reflected on Greene's habit of always giving his enemies the most convincing word, I thought he might be offering a kind of practice that anyone could learn from. We're so eager to think of enemies, I wrote—was I thinking of myself? Or, more likely, of my father? Or even Simon?—simply because we know, deep down, that the only real enemy is the one who keeps us closest company with every breath. It wasn't the country, the girl, the teacher who let us down; it was our judgment, and whatever led us to expect too much of the country, the girl or the teacher in the first place. That was why it became harder and harder to condemn anyone: wouldn't God himself, faced with a wounded murderer, feel somewhat at a loss?

I called my piece "Sleeping with the Enemy" and wrote about how Greene's special grace—his curse—was to see "the folly and frailty of everyone around him." It's never external devils that undo us, I suggested, but rather the ones that rise up in ourselves and those people who have the power to awaken them within us. Greene was "never a truer Christian," I concluded, "than when forgiving even his un-Christian enemies."

A few weeks later, the piece appeared on the back page of *Time* magazine, as most of my pieces had been appearing for the last nine years. I went to Japan again, and then came back, bringing my seventy-three-year-old future father-in-law for a trip through California, his first visit to the country that had opposed him as a soldier in the war and wiped out his hometown of Hiroshima. I returned to my desk and started working on another piece, on Los Angeles's airport, and the way the empires of old had been usurped. Then, coming upstairs in the rebuilt house, I noticed the red light flashing on my phone.

I pushed the PLAY button to pick up the message and heard a voice I couldn't quite place, and then a kind of choking sound, then many long seconds of silence, before the receiver at the other end was put down. I pressed the button again, and this time I realized it was my father's voice. He almost never rang me up and, when he did, it was usually to talk about some book he'd recently discovered—*The Honourable Schoolboy* or the autobiography of Marlon Brando. This time, though—I could only just make out—he was saying something about having seen my essay on Graham Greene, "Sleeping with the Enemy," and how . . . and then his voice gave out and he began to sob.

I couldn't ever remember hearing him sob before, least of all over an answering machine. It was a shocking thing, to hear a man famous for his fluency and authority lose all words. Something had obviously touched him, or devastated him in the Greenian theme of being unable to look anywhere but to oneself for blame. The sound of his racking sobs continued, and then there was that silence—I couldn't guess what was happening—and the phone put down.

I met him and my mother a few weeks later, on a bright, warm day in late May—was it pain I saw in his eyes, the sense of something he could never put behind him?—and then I flew back to my new home in Japan. On one of my first days there, a call came in the dead of night: my father was in the critical care unit, with pneumonia, and things didn't look good. I flew back the next day and saw him in his bed, stirring, but not obviously conscious, his feet sticking up in just the odd way mine did. Ten days later, he was dead, at sixty-five, and the last real time I'd heard from him was the gasping call about Graham Greene.

∴

I couldn't quite explain to Hiroko, as I was finishing this book, which man within my head I was addressing. "You're writing about your father?" she said, with genuine, alert curiosity one morning as the sun came up above a thick late-autumn mist. "Well, not exactly. There's too much I don't know—or could never say—about him." "But Graham Greene. You like him?" "Yes." I couldn't quite convey even to her how difficult it was at times to read *The Quiet American:* I'd pick up my worn orange copy with the pages beginning to separate from their binding, and I'd see a brash American reaching out for support, or Fowler calling the man he's more or less condemned to death his "friend" (perhaps his only friend), or see him trying to petition his wife for a divorce and realizing, at the very end, that, as Teresa of Avila had it, more tears are shed over answered prayers than unanswered, and I couldn't say why it struck me with such force. "There are no bad guys in his books," I told her. "But no one's entirely good either. There can't be final resolutions, least of all happy ones; yet people are moving, even heroic, precisely because they don't always live down to our fears for them. It's like what you learn in your Buddhism: that if you see how even the guy you think you dislike is suffering, it becomes harder to think so badly of him. But harder, too, sometimes, to hope for clarity or permanence."

Then I looked up, to see the tiny, characterless apartment, in this deeply impenetrable land, the woman whose language was so different from my own—Phuong never answers Fowler's questions, so he has to learn to read her silences (or, more often, strategically not to do so)—and the masks from various old countries on the wall, and thought of one other person who could settle down here, for a time, and find diversion in the very foreignness.

∴

It was New Year's again, and Louis and I were in the little town of Sucre in southern Bolivia, where squat men with squarish faces were smearing their giggling children with confetti, and girls in their best pink dresses were glancing nervously at boys on the second floor of a bar above the town square ("No, Louis," I said, "you're too old"). We'd just had a long candlelit dinner in a courtyard among the brightly colored colonial buildings, catching up after a few years apart, and he was telling me about some of the places he'd visited recently (Romania, Albania, Mozambique) and I was seeing between the lines the emergency rations of food, or at least support, he was taking to people in these stricken worlds. I'd invited him to come and spend a few days together in Bolivia because it seemed to me the hidden jewel of the Americas, the most primal, intriguingly spooky place I'd found in my thirty years of crisscrossing the continent. Miners were said to worship the devil in the nearby towns, and at festivals, I'd read, the true spirit of the country came out from behind the impassive exterior.

"Tomorrow Potosí!" I said, and he said, "Sure." The highest town in the world, at thirteen thousand feet, was only three hours away by car, and it was said to be a spectacular road, winding over high mountains and then passing across areas so remote that not even much Spanish was spoken there (only a version of the Indian language Quechua). There was a terrible aspect to the situation—the UN had found rural poverty in Bolivia the worst on the planet (ninety-seven percent of people in parts living below the poverty line)—but it was in places of privation, I knew, that Louis felt the greatest capacity to serve; Belgravia had less need of what he had to offer.

"Eight o'clock breakfast?" I said, as we walked down the narrow cobbled street to our small hotel, our footsteps echoing behind us as we left the revelry of the main square behind.

"Sounds good. I'll bring my backgammon set. Some tapes."

"You reserved the car?"

"Twice. The girl at the front desk said it would be there at nine o'clock."

I'd already called Hiroko in Japan, in the middle of a lavish New Year's festival, and my mother in California; as ever, they'd see me in the next week or two, when my assignment was over. "It's magical," I told Hiroko, when she asked me why I'd go back to a place where my passport had been confiscated the previous time I'd come here, to write about it again. "It's like traveling into a medieval world where the old forms are very strong. Undiluted. Raw."

We finished breakfast quickly the next morning and talked about the celebrations of the night before. They had been as simple, as unpretentious, as full of innocent humanity as Bolivia often seemed to be; most of the people around us, I imagined, were now sleeping off the late night, the drink, the dancing, perhaps the coca leaves they'd been chewing to stay awake.

A man plodded up to us, a smiling, quiet man from the hotel who had taken us to our broken rooms the day before.

"Potosí?" he said, and we nodded, and he led us outside.

At that moment, a car came screeching down the narrow, silent street and a boy jumped out. He couldn't have been more than nineteen, but in his tomato-red T-shirt, his wrap-around shades, the borrowed accent he affected, he looked like the face of the new Bolivia.

"Hi, guys," he said in English, not a language much spoken in these parts. "I'm taking you to Potosí."

"No," said the older man, and a dispute broke out.

"Look," said the kid, and handed us a voucher. Clearly the woman at the desk had made the reservation twice, but the boy spoke English and had a voucher, and perhaps the older man would be glad of the chance to spend New Year's Day with his family, even if he missed out on the payment.

We got into the car, and Louis handed over an ancient cassette of the Jefferson Airplane.

"Hey, Woodstock!" said the boy, turning round to grin and give us the thumbs-up sign. "Crosby, Stills, Nash and Young! Jimi Hendrix!"

He jammed the cassette in—we were a long way now from the broken Toyota in Ethiopia—and Grace Slick began wailing about how one pill makes you larger and one pill makes you small. He reversed at high speed down the block and then started gunning the car around the cobbled, ancient streets.

"You speak English," I said, incisively, as "Feed your head" screamed around us.

"Why not?" He turned around as he drove and smiled enormously again. His tangled mass of dark curls shook with the cacophonous music.

Very soon—the tires squealed as the boy rounded turns—we were in the countryside, and within minutes, so it seemed, the town was behind us, as were most signs of civilization. Then we were high up in the mountains—more than twelve thousand feet above sea level—and on one side was a sheer drop that fell what looked to be eleven thousand of those feet.

"Lucky we didn't choose 'the most dangerous road in the world,'" I said. The Lonely Planet guide had described, with some relish, a mountain road not far away on which an average of twenty-six vehicles a year veered over the edge, to fall three thousand feet to a valley floor. Modern vehicles in a largely undeveloped place like Bolivia are always an uncertain proposition, and even the road we drove along now was lined with the small white crosses and simple memorials, sometimes draped in fresh flowers, that remembered inattentive drivers or unlucky passengers.

"Did I tell you about my friend Harri?" I asked.

"No."

"You met him almost thirty years ago, the first time you came to Santa Barbara. One of the nicest guys I ever knew in California. We used to play tennis together—for years—and he was the ideal partner: he never wanted to win, and we were always at exactly the same level. We'd start playing again after years apart, and every set would end in a tiebreaker. I played the piano—Bach—when he got married in our house, thirty-five years ago. As the sun came up. Not long before we did 'The Rape of the Lock' with Meredith."

"Really?" I could tell my friend was more interested, understandably, in Grace Slick.

We came to slightly flatter land, and the car began to bump, then to rattle as it bounced along a track just off the side of the road, next to a ditch.

"You okay?" I shouted.

The driver swiveled round. "No problem!"

We continued on our way and then, out of nowhere, he pulled up at a gas station.

"One moment," he said, and disappeared.

"He's strange," I said to Louis.

"More than strange."

"Sinister almost."

"More than sinister."

It only hit me now that the boy probably hadn't slept much on New Year's Eve; for all we knew, he might still have some drink, or coca, in his system. But going back would be as dangerous as going forwards, and we hadn't wanted to bother the older man.

"You sure you're okay?" I said, as he came back. He hadn't filled up the car or done anything with it at all.

He gave the thumbs-up sign again and turned the volume on the Airplane way up.

We started to climb once more—another pass—and every now and then the car bumped off the tarmac, to the side, or seemed to waver around the central line. Luckily, few other cars were visible in rural Bolivia at 10:00 a.m. on New Year's Day.

"Anyway, Harri, whom I was just telling you about, got killed in a car crash, four months ago. It was the strangest thing; I mean, he was the one who'd taught me how to drive. He'd been driving—everywhere—for forty years. But he had a new wife, from Russia, and she was at the wheel, on a freeway in Utah, and somehow she rolled the car. He was thrown out and killed. She was almost fine, though she wasn't wearing a seat belt either. And ever since . . ."

And then I noticed that we were careening, at high speed, into the mountainside.

"Jesus Christ!" I screamed, and the driver, jolted awake, swerved crazily to try to avoid the rock face. But it was too late, and we slammed into the mountain, and then bounced back. The car fell on its top and righted itself. Then, just as things seemed to settle down, we began to bounce once more, into a ditch and then back out again, onto our side.

"Why is he trying to kill us?" had run senselessly through my head in the long seconds before the actual collision. "What has he got against us? Why has he come here to get rid of us?" Instinctively getting into a fetal position as I saw the collision imminent, I might have been preparing to go out of the world in much the same way I had come into it.

Now, as the car stopped bouncing, there was silence everywhere. After a long, long time, I said, "Are you all right?" I heard a groan from somewhere.

Scrunching even further down, no longer human, I slithered through a shattered window and got haltingly up. Everywhere there was blood and glass. The carry-on that had been in the locked trunk was now in a ditch twenty feet away. Cassettes and sunglasses and shorts that had been inside it were scattered across the road. A tape that had come unspooled. Louis's worn Bible. A hat he'd brought to protect himself from the sun.

I didn't know what to do, so, reflexively, senselessly, I began clambering around, collecting the stuff from the ditch. Then Louis came out. Blood was pouring down his face, as if he'd just walked out of a scene from *The Texas Chainsaw Massacre*.

"Are you okay?"

"I don't think so."

Too many seconds later, the driver wriggled out through the windscreen. He was cradling a bloody mess of an arm and wailing like a baby.

I walked around collecting the stray tapes, the sunglasses, the backgammon set that had accompanied us to so many places.

"It's okay," said Louis. "I don't think I'll be wanting that cassette again very soon."

No cars at all were visible, thankfully—on a regular day drivers would have been veering around us and into one another's paths—but we were alone on a silent mountain road in southern Bolivia at twelve thousand feet.

We waited and waited—I picked up more stuff—when, suddenly, as we hobbled across the tarmac, a car appeared around a turn, a bright SUV (the last kind of vehicle you'd expect on such a road), and a man jumped out. In a grey sweater, pressed trousers, startlingly clean for an area where not even Spanish was spoken and almost everyone lacked the barest essentials of life.

"¿Qué pasa?" he said. And then, more startling still, with what seemed to be a natural take-charge manner, he turned to us and spoke directly. "You speak English? What happened?" He looked to be a lawyer or the prosperous head of some local company, though what he was doing on this deserted road I couldn't imagine.

I explained the situation. "I will take you to a hospital," he said. "Can you move?"

"Is it far away?"

"Not far. One hour. More. Come." He led Louis to the backseat of his new car and sat him very upright. I sat by my friend and thought back on our adventure in Ethiopia.

"What about the driver?"

"He is okay. He must stay here for the police. They will take him to the hospital in Potosí."

The car started up, and, as the man accelerated over a bump, Louis let out a shout of involuntary pain.

"I'm sorry. I will go slower."

"Please."

It seemed like so many trips we had taken together; I was the one left to talk to the driver, while Louis tried to nurse himself back to normalcy. We had been in that accident in rural Cuba I sometimes thought about—he'd hit a boy on a bicycle while driving too fast—and I remembered the time he'd hit a dog in Morocco. He'd only had to visit me in California once to end up in a rural hospital near Nevada with dysentery. "How are you?" I'd said when we'd met four days earlier in the Plaza Hotel in La Paz. "Great," he'd said. "Just give me time."

"So," the driver now said, as we again climbed up the mountain road, reversing our tracks, "you are from England."

"Yes. We were at school together, years ago."

"I was in Blackpool for three weeks," the driver said. "Learning English."

"Really?"

"When I was studying in Rome."

We continued a little farther, and I could feel how every turn and pothole was throwing my friend out of joint; he sat as still as an Egyptian statue in a museum.

"You know this place, Eton?"

"Yes. Very well."

"I went to see it when I went to Windsor Castle," said the driver. All that studying of English, and he could not have had many chances to use it.

"You're in business?"

"Business?" He laughed. "I am the Bishop of Potosí. I am going to Sucre now to conduct the Mass for New Year's Day."

Hadn't Greene written about some bishop of San Luis Potosí in *The Lawless Roads*? But even in his books it seemed implausible that a savior on a deserted road would be a man of the cloth.

"We're lucky you came along."

"It's not luck," the bishop said. "It's a miracle."

An hour passed, another half an hour, and there was no sign of a clinic.

"Maybe it would be better to go back to Sucre?"

"No. We must get your friend to a hospital soon. I know a place."

It had been two hours now, but maybe, I thought, he was driving slowly so as not to jolt Louis too violently?

Finally, he turned off the main road, and we were bouncing along the barely paved paths of a village, and the bishop was parking outside a small blue house.

"One moment," he said, and disappeared.

Minutes later he reemerged, with a very pretty young girl by his side, in a fluffy pink dress. She sat next to him in the front, very straight, and I wondered who this teenage companion was. A daughter, as in the story of the runaway priest I'd written in Easter Island? An altar girl, perhaps? A local guide?

I didn't want to entertain the other options—the Greenian ones—as she directed the bishop down a small road, out of town, till we arrived at a squat, single-story building. The clinic—as some words on a wall announced—had been established by the British to help Bolivia. Three Indian women in bowler hats were sitting stoutly outside, looking, as they often do in Bolivia, as if they had been sitting there, accepting and almost motionless, for centuries.

We walked inside, and the nurse on duty let out a gasp, her mouth flying open when she saw Louis, the rivers of blood running down his face. She led us to a small bare room and told him to sit on the bed. A friendly man with a round face appeared, with a flyswatter, to keep the insects away.

A few minutes later a young doctor arrived—interrupted, no doubt, in his New Year's Day lunch, but capable and brisk. He spoke Spanish at least.

"Your friend can understand what I say?"

"Not a word."

"Tell him, please, that I have to make some stitches in his head. Fifteen, maybe more. He must sit very still. I don't have anesthetic."

It might have been the Indian in Mérida again: what was this doctor doing in this far-off village? Fulfilling some sense of duty or escaping an unburied secret in the city? I told Louis to be a man, as we'd been taught at school, and warned him that it would hurt, eliminating some of the details. He cried out in pain, and I sat by the bed and held his hand.

Then it was over, and the bishop and his pretty friend made their farewells.

"We must take him in an ambulance to Sucre," said the doctor. Louis was placed on a gurney and carried out to a little van. I noticed, as we left, the big board at the front of the clinic, advertising prices. An IV cost twelve cents. A night's stay would cost twenty cents. An ambulance would set us back fifteen cents. The three women in bowler hats couldn't go in, I guessed, because the prices were too high.

The ambulance started up—sirens wailing and lights

flashing—and I sat in the back with my prostrate friend. "The worst of it is over," I said, like a parody of myself.

"I hope so. It's a miracle we're even here."

At ten, maybe fifteen miles an hour, the van labored over the unpaved roads, and, forty-five minutes later, we pulled up at a small hospital in Sucre. Louis was taken into a room with fourteen other beds, each one occupied by a man who looked as if he had been bashed about the head, by the police or their enemies. Some of the men were wailing, loudly. Some were ominously quiet. A nurse came in and tried to help, but it was difficult with a patient who spoke no Spanish.

I tried to translate for a doctor as he said, "I think your friend is okay. But we must keep him here. For observation. One week."

"A week?"

"It is important."

One of the men in the room let out a rending cry. Young women and children came and stood round some of the beds. Someone said that the mother and sister of our driver were on their way. They wanted to pay for us. Words like "hemorrhage" and "infection" and "fracture" were hard for me in Spanish.

Abruptly, someone decided that Louis needed a brain scan. There was said to be a machine for this in another hospital in Sucre. But night had begun to fall by the time he was carried out of the bare room with green walls on a gurney and put into an ambulance again to be taken to a sleeker facility up the hill.

On arrival, we were whisked into a high-tech radiation room, and he was put on a bed. A button was pushed, and slowly he disappeared inside a shell.

"Come," said a young nurse. "You can watch."

I joined her in the booth next to the machine and we

saw a diagram of my friend's head. "So," she said—she had identified herself as "Anna"—"this is his skull. No, wait, this is his cranium. No, maybe this is a line on the screen of the machine . . ."

"Maybe you could ask a doctor to take a look?"

"I am a lab technician. The only one. No doctor here can read these."

"Is there someone in the capital?"

Her face lit up. "Of course! I will e-mail the scan to someone in La Paz." She pushed a few buttons on the ultramodern machine. "Okay. Maybe fax."

She printed out a copy of the scan—there were lines all over his skull, and she seemed to know as little as I did about what any of them meant—and then went to a nearby machine. "I'm sorry," she said. "The fax machine is broken."

She fiddled around with it some more—someone else had now wheeled Louis back to the ambulance—and then, as if on cue, the electricity went out. Anna and I were alone in the dark, with a printout of my friend's brain.

We edged through the room in the pitch blackness, bumping against the bed, what might have been a computer, an expensive piece of equipment. "Oh, sorry!" "Is that you?" "No, you're here . . ."

She got to the door and opened it. The whole space was black. Outside, all of Sucre was quiet and dark, too. Clearly, lights had gone off across the city.

Far down the hallway, a woman was standing with a candle, talking to a man in a white coat. Anna led me down the corridor and, stopping the doctor with a firm, gentle hand on the arm, she held the scan (upside down, I think) and said, "You think it's okay?"

"Sure," he said. "Why not?" And hurried off to some more urgent matter.

We got into the ambulance and took Louis back to where he had been placed before.

∴

So," said Anna, after accompanying us back to the room of wailing men. It was still New Year's Day. "You would like dinner?"

She felt sorry for me, I could tell, and though I longed to return to my room and nurse my wounds—my legs were aching and my body was stiff, and I wanted to call Hiroko and hear the solace of her voice—it seemed cruel to abandon our new friend after all her hard work. We sat in a little cafeteria, and she told me of her dreams of practicing medicine, of how difficult everything was in Bolivia, of her hobby, singing. In some ways I might have been with the sweet tour guide in Lake Titicaca from my previous trip: Anna could not have been less pushy, kinder, more innocent in what she hoped for. She still lived with her parents, though close to thirty, and when we walked out into the street close to midnight, she said, "I will see you in the hospital at nine a.m. tomorrow" and got onto a bus home with a welcome lack of fuss, waving to me from the window.

The next day she was as good as her word. She spoke to the doctors. "Of course they say he must stay. They want a rich foreigner in their bed. There is no need. They are criminals, all of them." She explained to the driver's grieving mother and small sister that we were touched, deeply touched, by their gesture, but we could afford the five dollars the stay would cost. In the night, Louis told us, he had cried out for help, the pain was so intense. But the nurse had refused to give him even an aspirin. Of course, Anna said: you had to pay for medication in advance, and an aspirin could cost a cent. They didn't want you to get one free.

It seemed wise to try to get away from the place, if only to the capital. Anna helped find us seats on a flight out at lunchtime. She called to La Paz to locate a hospital that would take Louis, an international facility in the embassy district. She called to double-check that an ambulance would be waiting for us when we landed. At Sucre's little airport, she accompanied us to the tiny office where a man ensured that Louis was fit to fly.

When we got to Sopocachi, and a truly sleek facility in La Paz, with a doctor who spoke English, Louis asked if it had been madness to get on a plane.

"Yes," said the doctor, matter-of-factly.

"So if there was a problem, I could have . . ."

"Yes. It was very stupid."

Then we managed to get flights out of the country, back to the safety of our homes, and the letters from Anna, kind and imploring ("You know how it is in Bolivia"), began to stream in.

∴

I still bear scars, visible and less so, from our accident in Bolivia; somehow the world it opened onto was so charged and dark, so far from logic, that I cannot easily leave it behind.

Driving up hairpin turns in the Indian foothills of the Himalayas three months later, the boys at the wheel accelerating wildly around blind switchbacks, I had to close my eyes, gripping the seat between my knuckles, because I could feel it all happening again. My house burned down as I watched, I was in a car in Egypt that ran over a little boy in a village—his bloody body thrown into our backseat so that there were stains all over—I have seen close friends possessed or try to commit suicide; but none of that so unnerved me, or haunts me still, as the boy in the tomato-red T-shirt. The modern world has yet to make many inroads on Bolivia—that was why I wanted to share it with Louis—and it was possible to believe, as Greene had believed in places like Liberia and Haiti, that one was back in a much more potent world where none of our easy defenses or learned reflexes could help us.

It was not fashionable to believe all that; I'd resisted such implications for most of my life. It was exactly what we had been trained to disbelieve at school, even as we were being taught about a man walking on water and offering his body for us to eat, rising from the dead and turning water into wine. Most English literature, if it stuck resolutely enough to the social, could pretend that devils (and certainly gods) didn't exist, and it was always easier to think so. Religion, in that sense, was part of the way Greene rebelled against his upbringing, affirming the subconscious. It wasn't faith that was the escape, he always maintained, but atheism. Yet he had seen and traveled enough to have an acute, almost obsessive sense of the limits of what we can explain or know, and to realize that darkness can be more important to acknowledge than light, precisely because we are so happy to discount its existence.

Besides, an adopted father can never die, I thought again;

that's one of the great advantages he has over a real one. Indeed, if he's departed the world already, a virtual or a chosen father need never even age; he's always at the stage you need him to be, and you can hold him in all his ages at the same time, if you so choose. He grows old as you do, the books ripening and taking on new colors, so that what once seemed comical gathers shadows all around it. Yet he never grows too old, or loses his memory. He's always there for you. Like a god, Greene might have added—except that a human, faltering, contradictory god is sometimes easier to believe in.

∴

When I went to the last room my father ever occupied—it turned out to be on the same road where I was sleeping, though down in the flats, while I was in the mountains—I saw his books arranged by his seat on the floor, where he liked to reach for them, and the mass of yellow, sky blue, grey folders that he always kept, with horoscopes, photocopies, caduceus symbols, records of important documents stashed inside them. His ashtray was on the table, and the pack of cigarettes that had in fact brought him to his death was sitting there, waiting to be opened. He had died not many days before, and it fell to me to sort his things out.

As I was going through the books he kept beside him, heavily marked up, I saw that he was reading Gandhi, as ever, his chosen father, and was also collecting books (perhaps he'd always collect these more than read them) on how to improve his health. Then I saw, to my astonishment, a cover that looked familiar, and noticed that it was a copy of the first book I'd ever written, in the old, burned-down house, while he was still wondering if there was evil in California.

I opened it and found it as marked up as any of his old books of philosophy or poetry might have been: heavy double underlinings in some places, cryptic arrows or infinity signs in red and black in the margin; parentheses that denoted some intense response beside the words. I couldn't tell what the feeling was exactly, but he seemed to have devoured my book as intensely, with as much rigor, and even approval, as if it were a copy of *The Republic* or Kant's *Critique of Pure Reason*. Then I went into his bedroom, where his slippers sat by the bed, as if waiting for him to get out from under the covers and slip off to the bathroom.

There were a few more volumes by his bedside—maybe company for the night—and one of them, I saw to my amazement, was another copy of that first book, which couldn't have been the easiest one for a father to delight in with its raucous and heedless adventures across ten countries in the East.

In all its 378 pages, there was only one marking: at the top of one page, my father had carefully copied out a sentence I'd cited from Proust, "The real paradises are the paradises lost."

A son may choose never to listen to a father, but a father, as Greene saw as well as anyone, is always bound to a son, and real disinheritance is hard. Another advantage virtual fathers have.

In the time left to me," Greene had written in his letter, after I'd asked if he might be willing to sit still for a profile in *Time* magazine, and the phrase had stuck with me, haunting, as the words of those in their eighties often are. Even though more and more of his stories, as he went on, are set in autumn, one of the main occupations of his characters is to see how far they've come, or fallen rather, since the spring. Yet insofar as spring—youth—is visible, there's always the possibility of vicarious renewal or hopefulness, and the mixed feelings of seeing someone else's perhaps too-innocent illusions.

His inability to trust himself would not have mattered if he hadn't so hungered for peace, and his longing for peace would not have been so poignant if it hadn't been his unquiet mind that always kept him from finding it. "From childhood I had never believed in permanence," Fowler says, "and yet I had longed for it."

There weren't many things I still had to ask him; his life was an open book, he'd laid himself so naked to the world on the page. If I met my father I might have asked—though perhaps something would always prevent me from broaching the difficult stuff—"How much did you really believe? What is it that most compels you? Where do the lines of faith run in you and where do they stop?" But with Greene there'd be no need of words at all. He knew me better than I did myself. I knew him better than I knew Louis or my father or many of the people closest to me, when it came to his secrets, his sins, his most intimate needs. I closed the door of my father's final temporary residence and got back into my car to drive up the hill, to where a rebuilt house, no longer yellow, sat alone on a ridge, and a quiet American, inside a faded orange book, was ready to keep me company with talk about the importance of never mocking innocence too readily—and the snarls that invariably turn around compassion.

ACKNOWLEDGMENTS

Thank you, first of all, to my dear old friend (and sometime editor) Louise Dennys, who, along with her late sister, Amanda, and brother Nicholas (all following in the footsteps of their mother, Elisabeth), has done so much to keep alive the legacy of her uncle Graham, and with her husband, Ric Young, has passed so much of Greene's memory down to the rest of us; to my old colleague Bernard Diederich, for remaining so staunch a protector of his longtime friend, and for sharing with me, over many years, talk of their adventures together; and to my newer friends Paul Theroux and Michael Mewshaw, for offering glimpses into the older writer who took them in and showed them kindness. And thank you, of course, to the late Norman Sherry, for his untiring work of biographical excavation, to which this book, as so many others, is transparently indebted.

Thank you to my old school friend Louis, for showing me, amidst so much else, how belief in God could be not just a namby-pamby, Sunday Schoolish kind of thing, but a catalyst to deeply engaged, thoughtful compassion in the world, extended even to such half believers as me; to U2, for some of the same; and to Sigur Rós, for offering a glimpse of peace and clarity without the clutter of personality. And thank you to the monks of New Camaldoli, for providing shelter, warm friendship, silence and, most of all, a vision of surrender to so many of us caught up in the storms of the world.

Thank you to everyone at Alfred A. Knopf, my books' first home for more than a quarter of a century now, starting with my literary godfather, Sonny Mehta, and my editor, Dan Frank, who has, so searchingly and tenaciously, over five books now, pushed me to go deeper and closer to the bone, then come up with dozens of inspired textual suggestions; to my old friends at the company, among them Marty Asher, Robin Desser, Pam Henstell, Sheila Kay, Nicholas Latimer and the brilliant jacket designer Abby Weintraub; and to my irreplaceable friend and agent, Lynn Nesbit, as well as to Cullen Stanley, among many other stalwart protectors at Janklow & Nesbit Associates.

Thank you, finally, to Hiroko, for more than everything, and to my mother, for all the things I've long forgotten and failed to thank her for, and thank you to the author who, almost in spite of himself, taught me and so many others how to move around the world and even how to hazard trust—especially when the evidence may be against it.

A NOTE ABOUT THE AUTHOR

Pico Iyer has written nonfiction books on globalism, Japan, the Fourteenth Dalai Lama and forgotten places, and novels on Revolutionary Cuba and Islamic mysticism. He regularly writes on literature for *The New York Review of Books,* on travel for the *Financial Times* and on global culture and the news for *Time, The New York Times* and magazines around the world.

A NOTE ON THE TYPE

This book was set in Caledonia, a Linotype
face designed by W. A. Dwiggins (1880–1956).
It belongs to the family of printing types
called by printers "modern face"—a term used
to mark the change in style of the type letters
that occurred around 1800.

TYPESET BY
Scribe, Philadelphia, Pennsylvania

PRINTED AND BOUND BY
R. R. Donnelley, Harrisonburg, Virginia

DESIGNED BY
Iris Weinstein